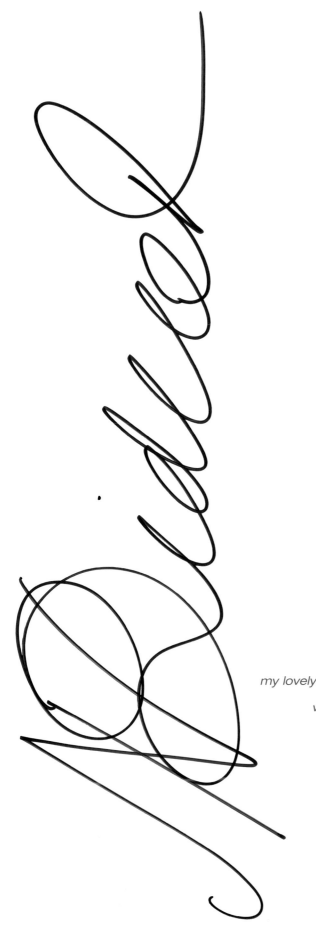

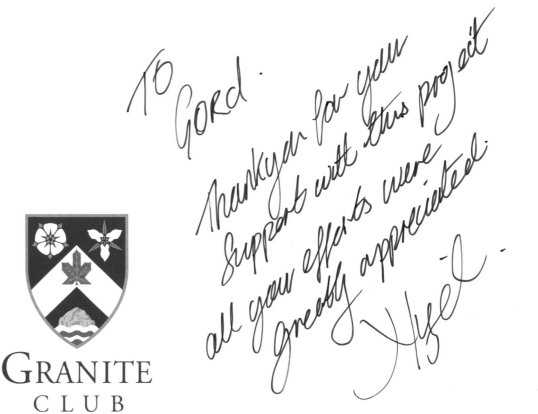

To Gord.
Thank you for your
support with this project
all your efforts were
greatly appreciated.

GRANITE CLUB

Tradition, Heritage, Family,

Sportsmanship, Camaraderie

To the Granite Club,

for their appreciation of the

finer things in life.

For Grandfather,

my lovely French wife, Catherine, and son, Sébastien,

who gave me the gifts of inspiration,

encouragement and

understanding.

GRANITE CLUB

On a warm summer day in 1875, five Toronto businessmen combined

the basic ingredients that would become the recipe for the Granite Club.

Canada's first prime minister, Sir John A. Macdonald, accepted the

position of the Toronto Granite Curling Club's first honorary patron.

On Robbie Burns Day, January 25, 1876, the founders established the

Club's constitution. On the first Annual Club Day, the 5th of February

that year, following a feisty bonspiel between the "Old Countrymen"

and the "Canadians," the members sat down to a traditional curling

dinner of "beef and greens and bannocks...delicious mince collops and

stomach-tying haggis...with some pretty, tiny, kickshaws thereafter to

fill up...the interstices of appetite. Scottish beer in stone bottles and

"'alf and 'alf" in pewter mugs helped wash it all down." So began the

Granite Club, formulated on a passion for curling and nurtured on

traditional Scottish fare.

In the early 1900s a new ingredient was added — women were invited to join! Members were soon enjoying skating, lawn tennis, lawn bowling, billiards, whist, hockey, alley bowling and soon, swimming, badminton, hand ball, squash and golf would be added to the mixture. The family orientation of the Club solidified. In 1937, Gordon Sinclair wrote "Never have I...seen a spot where the whole family can play at some game suitable to their age and temperament and do it in the same building at the same time." Dining and entertaining became an important component of club life, as the Club regularly played host to important dinners, dances and receptions.

Capturing the Spirit is a celebration of the Granite Club's culinary evolution, from a single ingredient — a gentlemen's sports club — to a truly unique institution, providing an annual roster of feasts and fun for generations of Toronto's most discerning citizens and families.

CHEF
NIGEL
DIDCOCK

Keen for adventure, I followed my grandfather to the greenhouse.

As he opened the door, I was struck by the intense aroma of

tomatoes. Once inside I was captivated by their variety, and by the

rows of English cucumbers hung perfectly straight. Beyond

Grandad's greenhouse stood a beautiful orchard, laden with fruit.

To the left lay a vegetable plot of neatly aligned rows, abundant with

beets, cabbages, leeks, carrots and rhubarb. Gran's kitchen was

full of delicious aromas — strawberry jam, followed by raspberry and

blackberry as the seasons progressed. Apple crumble and rhubarb

pies were plentiful. Homemade applesauce accompanied pork and

crackling, and roast potatoes were in abundance.

The foundation had been set. My grandfather had opened the door

to a passion that would fuel me forever — an appreciation of fine

produce and the infinite array of flavourful possibilities that could

ensue. In his earlier years my grandfather, Phillip John Didcock,

was a chef in the Royal Navy. Grandad also prepared meals on the

HMS Victory for heads of state and dignitaries such as Field Marshal

Viscount Montgomery and General Eisenhower. Could it be that one

day I, too, would be a chef?

On October 23, 1979, I entered the portal of the five-star Carlton Hotel.

My culinary journey had begun, an adventure that would lead me to

catering college and subsequently to London's Connaught Hotel

where I would meet my professional mentor, Chef Michel Bourdin.

Bourdin taught me the traditional skills required in the preparation of

fine French cuisine. When he deemed me to be ready, he ushered

me off to France to cultivate French sensibilities and be influenced by

the great masters of the Michelin and Relais & Châteaux circles —

George Paineau, Gérald Passédat, Paul Bocuse, and Pierre Troisgros.

Ten years later, an incredible opportunity brought me to Canada to

open Langdon Hall. I was finally ready to put into practice my many

years of culinary training and craftsmanship. Today, as Executive

Chef of the Granite Club, I am honoured to lead the culinary team in

Capturing the Spirit, creating food experiences for every club

occasion. It is my pleasure to share ideas and perhaps awaken

a passion in others as my grandfather did in me.

Scallops St. Jacques Provençale (recipe on page 18)

JANUARY
FEBRUARY
MARCH

Midwinter, long dark nights and cold days. Time to ponder new ideas

and revisit old traditions that bring light and warmth to the soul.

For me, it's open season for culinary delights. Seize the moment and

explore new flavours, be they spicy, sweet, savoury or salty.

Indulge in good conversation; sample a new wine or pour an old

favourite. Spend enjoyable evenings with friends, lingering at the table

after a great meal. Taking the time. Savouring the moment.

FINE DINING

Haute Cuisine, "classic cooking," is an art form. It takes time, a long

time. You move slowly and deliberately, with great attention to detail.

It is a source of pleasure, a sensory experience, the visual

presentation, aroma, texture and taste. I personally love the foie gras

au torchon preparation. It is luxurious, rare and expensive — visually

and texturally rich. Or, relish the flavours of wild hare. Imagine the

bustle in the kitchens of London's legendary Connaught during peak

game season. Have enthusiasm for crossing culinary boundaries and

revel in the great culinary adventure.

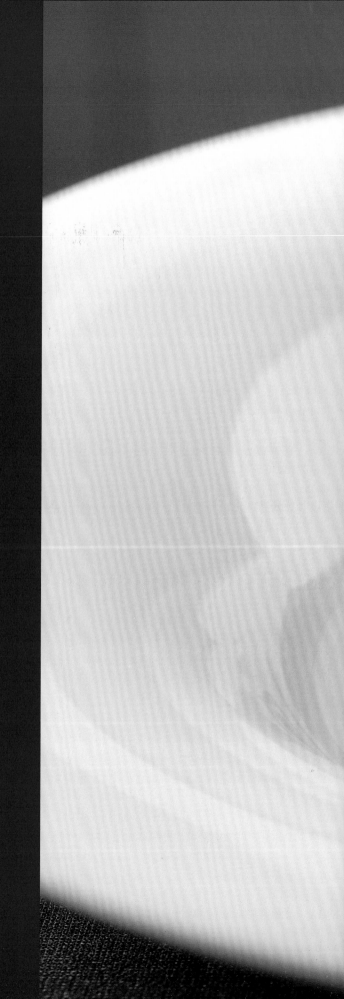

SCALLOPS ST. JACQUES PROVENÇALE

3 medium tomatoes
1/4 cup (50 mL) butter, clarified*
3 cups (750 mL) soft bread crumbs (4 large slices bread, crusts removed)
1 tsp (5 mL) finely chopped rosemary
1 tsp (5 mL) finely chopped thyme
18 live scallops in their shells (about 5 to 6 lb/2.5 to 3 kg)
1 tbsp (15 mL) olive oil
2 tbsp (25 mL) finely chopped shallots
3/4 cup (175 mL) white wine
Salt and pepper
Blanched seaweed or coarse salt (optional)

Remove stalks from tomatoes and cut a small X in the bottom of each one. In a saucepan of boiling water, blanch tomatoes for 30 seconds. Remove with a slotted spoon and immediately immerse in a bowl of ice water. When cool enough to handle, carefully peel tomatoes. Cut each tomato half crosswise; scoop out seeds and juices, and cut out stems. Put tomato halves cut sides down on paper towels to drain for 10 minutes. Chop finely; set aside in medium bowl at room temperature.

In a small skillet, heat clarified butter over medium heat. Add bread crumbs; cook for 6 to 8 minutes, stirring often, until crumbs are golden brown. Remove from heat; stir in half of rosemary and thyme.

Scrub scallops under cold running water, discarding any that don't close when tapped sharply on the counter. In a large stock pot, heat olive oil over medium heat. Add shallots; cook, stirring, for 3 minutes or until softened but not browned. Add scallops and wine; bring to a boil over high heat. Reduce heat to medium-high; cook, tightly covered, for 5 to 7 minutes until shells open. Remove from heat; let cool slightly.

Working with 1 scallop at a time and discarding any that haven't opened, tip any juices from scallop through a sieve set over a small bowl. With a small, sharp knife, carefully remove scallop (and its coral-coloured roe if any) from shell. Cut away and discard the circular muscle from each side of scallop and the dark grey sac. Put scallop with its roe in the deeper of its 2 shells, discarding flatter shell, and put scallop in shell on baking sheet. Repeat with remaining scallops. Tip reserved scallop juices back into pot.

Bring contents of pot back to a boil over medium-high heat; boil for 8 to 10 minutes, stirring often, until liquid has reduced to 1/4 cup (50 mL). Strain liquid through a fine sieve into bowl containing chopped tomatoes; stir in remaining rosemary and thyme. Season with salt and pepper to taste.

Preheat the broiler to high. Spoon tomato mixture over scallops, dividing evenly. Top with bread crumbs, dividing evenly. Broil 4 inches (10 cm) from heat for 2 to 3 minutes until golden brown. Line 6 plates with seaweed or coarse salt; divide scallop shells among plates.
Makes 6 servings

* To clarify butter, heat it in a small saucepan over medium-low heat until melted. Carefully skim off any foam, then slowly pour the clear butter into a small bowl, leaving its cloudy residue in the saucepan. Keep warm.

I like to use live scallops in their shells for this impressive appetizer and prefer the Pacific or Pec Nord varieties. If your fish store doesn't have these, substitute 18 regular sea scallops, pan-sear them in butter and olive oil for about 1 minute on each side, then divide among 6 individual shallow ovenproof dishes. Top scallops with the chopped tomatoes seasoned with 1/2 tsp (2 mL) each rosemary and thyme and salt and pepper to taste, then sprinkle with the sautéed bread crumbs before broiling. Ask for seaweed at your fish store; blanch and drain it before using.

GOLDEN-CRUSTED BLACK COD

with Chorizo-Leek Confit, Truffled Popcorn & Parsley Mustard Sauce

Chorizo-Leek Confit:

2 medium leeks (white and light green parts only)

1/2 cup (125 mL) Chicken Stock (page 217)

1 sprig thyme

1 tbsp (15 mL) olive oil

1 tbsp (15 mL) butter

Salt and pepper

6 oz (175 g) chorizo sausage

Truffled Popcorn:

3/4 cup (175 mL) unflavoured popped popcorn (2 tsp/10 mL unpopped corn)

1 tsp (5 mL) truffle oil

Salt and pepper

Parsley-Mustard Sauce:

1 tbsp (15 mL) olive oil

3 tbsp (45 mL) sliced shallots

1/4 cup (50 mL) white wine

1 cup (250 mL) Chicken Stock (page 217)

1 cup (250 mL) lightly packed, coarsely chopped parsley leaves and stems

1 tsp (5 mL) smooth Dijon mustard

1/3 cup (75 mL) butter, softened

Golden-Crusted Black Cod:

1 tbsp (15 mL) butter, clarified (page 18)

3/4 cup (175 mL) soft bread crumbs (1 large slice bread, crusts removed)

Salt and pepper

4 skinless, boneless black cod fillets (6 oz/175 g each)

1 tbsp (15 mL) olive oil

4 tsp (20 mL) grainy Dijon mustard

Chorizo-Leek Confit: Preheat the oven to 350°F (180°C). Wash leeks thoroughly under cold running water; drain well. Cut each diagonally into six 1/2 inch (1 cm) slices. In a shallow ovenproof dish, combine leeks, chicken stock and thyme; drizzle with olive oil, dot with butter and sprinkle with salt and pepper to taste. Bake, covered, for about 15 minutes until leeks are almost tender.

Meanwhile, trim ends from chorizo; cut diagonally into twelve 1/2 inch (1 cm) slices. Arrange chorizo slices on top of leeks. Bake, covered, for 5 to 10 minutes until chorizo is hot and leeks are tender. Keep warm.

Truffled Popcorn: In a medium bowl, toss popcorn with truffle oil. Season with salt and pepper to taste.

Parsley-Mustard Sauce: In a medium saucepan, heat oil over medium heat; cook shallots for 3 to 5 minutes, stirring often, until softened but not brown. Add white wine; simmer for 3 to 5 minutes until wine has almost all evaporated. Add chicken stock; bring to a boil over high heat. Boil for 5 to 7 minutes until liquid is reduced by half. Let cool slightly. In a blender (not a food processor), blend chicken stock mixture, parsley and mustard until parsley is finely minced. With motor running, gradually add butter a little at a time, until sauce is smooth and creamy. Strain sauce through a fine sieve; return to rinsed-out saucepan. Keep warm but do not boil.

Golden-Crusted Black Cod: Preheat the oven to 400°F (200°C). In a small skillet, heat clarified butter over medium heat. Add bread crumbs; cook for 3 to 5 minutes, stirring often, until crumbs are golden brown. Remove from heat; season with salt and pepper to taste.

Pat cod dry with paper towels; sprinkle lightly on both sides with salt and pepper. In a large, ovenproof skillet, heat oil over medium-high heat; sear fish for 2 minutes on each side until golden brown. Remove from heat. Spread mustard over top side of fish, dividing evenly. Top with bread crumbs, dividing evenly and pressing so crumbs adhere to fish. Transfer skillet to oven; bake for 5 minutes until flesh is flaking but still translucent in the centre.

To serve, remove chorizo from confit; divide among 4 plates. With a slotted spoon, spoon leeks over chorizo. Centre cod on chorizo-leek confit; top cod with popcorn, dividing evenly. Drizzle sauce around edge of each plate. *Makes 4 servings*

Moist, flaky black cod (a.k.a. sablefish) will literally fall apart if overcooked so watch it carefully toward the end of cooking time. The fish is done when the flesh just starts to flake but is still translucent in the centre.

VEAL MEDALLIONS

& Langoustine Tails with Morel Sauce & Sautéed Asparagus

Veal Medallions:
1-1/2 lb (750 g) veal tenderloin

Morel Sauce:
2 tbsp (25 mL) butter
8 oz (250 g) morels, cleaned and halved
1 tbsp (15 mL) finely chopped shallot
1/2 cup (125 mL) Chicken Stock, or less as required (page 217)
1 tbsp (15 mL) Cognac
1 tbsp (15 mL) Veal Jus (page 217)
1 cup (250 mL) whipping cream

Sautéed Asparagus:
20 stalks asparagus
1 tbsp (15 mL) olive oil
Salt and pepper

To Finish:
8 langoustines or large shrimp
Salt and pepper
2 tbsp (25 mL) butter
2 tsp (10 mL) olive oil
Pea shoots

Veal Medallions: Trim off any skinny ends of tenderloins (reserve trimmings for use in another recipe). With a small, sharp knife, trim off any silver skin from tenderloins by slipping the knife blade under it, angling blade slightly upward and cutting with a gentle back and forth motion. Wrap each tenderloin separately very tightly in plastic wrap, sealing ends well. Refrigerate for 24 hours.

Morel Sauce: In a medium skillet, heat 1 tbsp (15 mL) butter over medium-high heat. Add morels; cook, stirring often, for 6 to 8 minutes until golden and tender. Add shallot; cook, stirring, for 3 to 5 minutes until shallot is softened but not browned. Scrape contents of skillet into a fine sieve set over a bowl; set aside to drain for about 10 minutes. Pour any drained liquid from morels into a glass measure; add enough chicken stock to measure 1/2 cup (125 mL). If no liquid drains from mushrooms, use all chicken stock.

In a medium saucepan over medium heat, cook Cognac for 1 to 2 minutes until reduced to 1-1/2 tsp (7 mL). Add chicken stock mixture and veal jus; bring to a boil over medium-high heat. Boil for 3 to 5 minutes until reduced to about 1/4 cup (50 mL). Add cream; bring to a boil. Reduce heat to medium; boil for 10 to 12 minutes until sauce has reduced to 3/4 cup (175 mL) and is thick enough to coat the back of a spoon. Add morels; cook, stirring, for 1 to 2 minutes to heat through. Remove from heat; stir in remaining butter until melted. Season with salt and pepper to taste; keep warm but do not boil.

Sautéed Asparagus: Trim at least 1 inch (2.5 cm) from ends of asparagus, ensuring stalks are all the same length. With a vegetable peeler, peel skin from stem ends of asparagus. In a large skillet of boiling salted water, cook asparagus for 3 to 5 minutes until just tender. Drain well. Return to skillet; add olive oil and salt and pepper to taste. Toss well; keep warm.

To Finish: Preheat the oven to 400°F (200°C). With your fingers, break heads from langoustines, reserving 4 of the heads and discarding the rest. In a small saucepan of boiling water, blanch reserved heads for 2 minutes. With a slotted spoon, remove to a bowl of cold water; set aside. Peel langoustine tails by gently pinching the shell just above the ends of the tails then pulling gently to remove shells; set aside.

Unwrap tenderloin; cut crosswise into 8 even slices. Sprinkle veal medallions on both sides with salt and pepper. In a large ovenproof skillet, heat 1 tbsp (15 mL) butter and 1 tsp (5 mL) olive oil over medium-high heat. Add veal; sear for 3 minutes, turning once, until golden brown on both sides. Transfer skillet to oven; cook for 6 to 8 minutes for medium-rare.

Meanwhile, sprinkle langoustines with salt and pepper. In a small skillet, heat remaining butter over medium-high heat. Add langoustines; cook for 2 to 3 minutes, turning occasionally, until just firm.

To serve, arrange 2 veal medallions on each of 4 plates; top each portion with asparagus, dividing evenly. Spoon morel sauce onto each plate; garnish with pea shoots and reserved langoustine heads, brushing heads with remaining oil just before serving.
Makes 4 servings

If veal tenderloin is hard to find, substitute two 12 oz (375 g) pork tenderloins, cutting each into 4 medallions before cooking.

SEARED BEEF MEDALLIONS

with Balsamic Peppers, Pommes Abricotines & Sauce Poivre

Balsamic Peppers:
1 red sweet pepper

1 yellow sweet pepper

1 tbsp (15 mL) olive oil

1 tbsp (15 mL) balsamic vinegar

Salt and pepper

Pommes Abricotines:
1 large Yukon Gold potato (8 oz/250 g)

1 egg yolk

Salt and pepper

Vegetable oil for deep frying

1 tbsp (15 mL) flour

1 egg, beaten

1/4 cup (50 mL) panko bread crumbs

2 tbsp (25 mL) finely chopped almonds

Sauce Poivre:
1 tbsp (15 mL) drained, pickled
green peppercorns

1 tbsp (15 mL) brandy

1 cup (250 mL) Veal Jus (page 217)

1/4 cup (50 mL) whipping cream

1 tbsp (15 mL) butter, softened

Beef Medallions:
4 strip loin steaks (10 oz/300 g each)

Salt and pepper

Olive oil

1 lb (500 g) asparagus

Balsamic Peppers: Preheat the broiler to high. Cut peppers in half; arrange cut sides down on a parchment-paper-lined baking sheet. Broil 4 inches (10 cm) from broiler until skins are blackened and blistered all over. Transfer peppers to a bowl; cover tightly with plastic wrap and let stand for at least 10 minutes. When cool enough to handle, remove skin, seeds and white membrane from peppers; cut flesh lengthwise into thin strips.

Just before serving, heat oil in a medium skillet over medium-high heat. Add peppers; cook, stirring for 1 to 2 minutes until hot. Sprinkle with vinegar and season with salt and pepper to taste.

Pommes Abricotines: In a steamer set over a saucepan of simmering water, steam potato for 30 minutes until tender. Remove from heat. When cool enough to handle, remove skin. Pass potato through a ricer into a bowl (or rub through a fine sieve); stir in egg yolk, and salt and pepper to taste. Preheat the oven to 300°F (150°C). In a deep-fat fryer and following manufacturer's instructions, heat vegetable oil to 375°F (190°C). Alternatively, pour oil into a large, wide pot to a depth of 2 inches (5 cm); heat over medium-high heat until a candy thermometer registers 375°F (190°C). If using a pot, reduce heat as necessary to maintain correct temperature. Have ready a small, paper-towel-lined baking sheet.

Meanwhile, put flour on a plate; beat egg in a shallow dish. In a second shallow dish, stir together panko crumbs and almonds. Form potato mixture into 4 even-size balls. Roll potato balls in flour, then in beaten egg; roll in crumb mixture to coat completely. Carefully lower potato balls into hot oil; cook for 1-1/2 to 2 minutes, turning occasionally, until golden brown. Remove to prepared baking sheet; bake for 10 to 15 minutes until hot in the centre (check by piercing one ball with a slim knife). Keep warm.

Sauce Poivre: In a small saucepan, heat peppercorns and brandy over medium heat for a few seconds. Standing well back, set brandy alight. When flames have died down, add veal jus and cream; bring to a boil over high heat. Reduce heat to medium; boil for about 20 minutes until sauce has reduced to 1/2 cup (125 mL) and is thick enough to coat the back of a spoon. Remove from heat; whisk in butter. Season with salt and pepper to taste; keep warm but do not boil.

Beef Medallions: Trim excess fat from steaks; cut each in half crosswise, trimming pieces to form eight 4 oz (125 g) medallions (reserve any trimmings for use in another recipe). Pat medallions dry; sprinkle on both sides with salt and pepper. Heat a large, oiled, ridged grill pan over high heat. Sear medallions for 6 to 8 minutes, turning once, for medium-rare. Remove to a warm platter; tent loosely with foil and let rest for 5 to 10 minutes.

Meanwhile, trim at least 1 inch (2.5 cm) from ends of asparagus, ensuring spears are all the same length. With a vegetable peeler, peel skin from stem ends of asparagus. In a large skillet of boiling salted water, cook asparagus for 3 to 5 minutes until just tender. Drain well. Fan asparagus spears on each of 4 plates, dividing evenly. Set 2 medallions of beef on top of each portion of asparagus. Drizzle beef with sauce; pile peppers on top of beef. Serve with pommes abricotines.
Makes 4 servings

When the weather warms up, both the beef and sweet peppers can be cooked on the barbecue. Steaming the potato for the crispy, deep-fried pommes abricotines retains its fluffy, dry texture.

EFFILOCHADE OF WILD HARE

with Celery Root & Chestnut Purées

Effilochade:

2 wild hares (about 1-1/2 lb/750 g each)

4 cups (1 L) red wine

1 cup (250 mL) Chicken Stock (page 217)

1 cup (250 mL) Veal Stock (page 216)

1/2 cup (125 mL) coarsely chopped shallots

1 stalk celery, coarsely chopped

1 small carrot, coarsely chopped

1 whole head garlic, broken in half and loose papery skin discarded

2 tbsp (25 mL) tomato paste

10 dried juniper berries

1-1/2 tsp (7 mL) salt

1/2 tsp (2 mL) black peppercorns, cracked

2 bay leaves

1 sprig thyme

1 sprig rosemary

Celery Root Purée:

Half large celery root, peeled and cut into 1 inch (2.5 cm) pieces (1 lb/500 g)

Salt

1 bay leaf

1 small sprig thyme

1/4 cup (50 mL) whipping cream

Pinch grated nutmeg

Pepper

Chestnut Purée:

16 fresh chestnuts in their shells (8 oz/250 g)

1-1/2 cups (375 mL) Chicken Stock (page 217)

Half celery stalk, finely chopped

1 small sprig thyme

2 tbsp (25 mL) whipping cream

Salt and pepper

To Finish:

1 tbsp (15 mL) butter

1 tsp (5 mL) olive oil

Effilochade: In a large, non-reactive saucepan, combine front and back legs and saddle of hares (refrigerate the 4 fillets for use later), the red wine, chicken and veal stock, shallots, celery, carrot, garlic, tomato paste, juniper berries, salt, peppercorns, bay leaves, thyme and rosemary. Refrigerate, covered, for 24 hours.

Bring hare and marinade to a boil over high heat. Reduce heat to medium-low; simmer, partially covered, for 2 to 3 hours until back leg meat is very tender and pulls away from the bones. Remove from heat.

When cool enough to handle, strain contents of saucepan through a colander, reserving liquid and solids separately. Remove all meat from bones, shredding it finely; set meat aside in a medium bowl, discarding bones and remaining solids. Strain liquid through a fine sieve and return to clean saucepan. Bring to a boil over high heat. Reduce heat to medium; boil for about 20 minutes until liquid has reduced to 1 cup (250 mL). Season with salt and pepper to taste; pour over shredded meat. Let cool completely; refrigerate, covered.

Celery Root Purée: In a medium saucepan, combine celery root with enough salted water to cover; add bay leaf and thyme. Bring to a boil over high heat. Reduce heat to medium-low; simmer, covered, for 15 to 20 minutes until celery root is very tender. Drain well, discarding bay leaf. In a food processor, pulse celery root and thyme until smooth. Rub purée through a fine sieve, discarding solids in sieve. In rinsed-out saucepan, heat cream over medium heat until simmering. Stir in purée and nutmeg; season with salt and pepper to taste.

Chestnut Purée: With a small, sharp knife, cut a small strip of shell from 1 side of each chestnut. Put chestnuts in a medium saucepan of cold water. Bring to a boil over high heat; boil for 1 minute. Remove from heat. Working with 1 chestnut at a time, remove from saucepan with a slotted spoon; peel off shell and inner skin. Repeat with remaining chestnuts, dropping them back into hot water if they're difficult to peel.

Setting aside 4 nice-looking chestnuts for garnish, put remainder in a medium, shallow saucepan; add chicken stock, celery and thyme. Bring to a boil over high heat. Reduce heat to low; simmer, covered, for 30 to 40 minutes until chestnuts are very tender. Drain well, reserving cooking liquid.

In a food processor, pulse chestnut mixture until a stiff purée forms, adding a little of the reserved cooking liquid if purée is too thick to process. Rub purée through a fine sieve, discarding solids in sieve. In rinsed-out saucepan, stir together purée and cream over medium heat until hot; season with salt and pepper to taste.

To Finish: In a medium saucepan, reheat effilochade gently for 5 to 7 minutes, watching carefully to make sure it doesn't burn. Reheat purées in separate saucepans over medium-low heat. In a medium skillet, heat butter and oil over medium-high heat. With a small, sharp knife, remove any silver skin from hare fillets. Pat fillets dry with paper towels; sprinkle on both sides with salt and pepper. Cook for 1 to 2 minutes, turning once, until medium-rare. Slice hare fillets thinly on the diagonal. Mound effilochade on 4 plates. Arrange fillets around effilochade; drizzle with any additional sauce from effilochade. Spoon purées alongside; garnish with reserved chestnuts.
Makes 4 servings

An effilochade is a dish of braised shredded meat; the word comes from the French verb effilocher, *meaning "to fray." Order wild hares from your butcher and ask him to remove their front and back legs and cut the slim fillets from either side of the saddles, reserving all the butchered pieces and bones.*

Foie Gras Torchon (recipe on page 28)

FOIE GRAS TORCHON

with Icewine-Physalis Jelly

Foie Gras Torchon:

1 lb (500 g) fresh duck foie gras

1 tbsp (15 mL) icewine

1 tbsp (15 mL) brandy

1 tsp (5 mL) sugar

Salt and pepper

8 cups (2 L) Chicken Stock (page 217)

Icewine-Physalis Jelly:

6 oz (175 g) physalis, husks removed (about
1 cup/250 mL without husks)

3/4 cup (175 mL) icewine

2 tbsp (25 mL) packed brown sugar

2 tbsp (25 mL) Minus 8 icewine vinegar

2 tsp (10 mL) unflavoured powdered gelatine

6 physalis

Salad greens

Foie Gras Torchon: Remove foie gras from refrigerator; let stand at room temperature for 1 hour to make it more pliable.

Separate the foie gras into 2 lobes where it breaks naturally; place smooth side down on cutting board. Remove the most visible veins by gently pushing the flesh away from the veins and pulling the veins with the back of a small, sharp knife to release them. Try not to damage the smooth outer surface of the foie gras. Sprinkle both sides of foie gras with icewine, brandy, sugar, and salt and pepper to taste.

Lay an 18 inch (45 cm) square of double-layer cheesecloth on work surface. Arrange largest lobe of foie gras smooth side down crosswise on the cheesecloth and 2 inches (5 cm) from one edge; arrange any smaller pieces of foie gras that may have broken off on top; top with second lobe smooth side up. Roll foie gras very tightly in cheesecloth to enclose completely and form a sausage shape. Twist ends tightly; tie securely with kitchen string. Put on a plate; refrigerate for 30 minutes.

In a medium saucepan, bring chicken stock to a simmer over high heat. Put foie gras in a second medium saucepan wide enough to hold it; pour in enough hot chicken stock to cover foie gras completely (you may not need all the stock). Bring to a gentle simmer over medium heat; poach, covered, for 1-1/2 minutes. Remove foie gras from saucepan; put on wire rack over a large plate. Refrigerate for 15 minutes. Untie ends; twist very tightly and retie securely. Refrigerate on rack for 24 hours before serving.

Icewine-Physalis Jelly: Preheat oven to 300°F (150°C). Cut physalis into quarters. In a small baking dish, stir together physalis, icewine, sugar and icewine vinegar. Bake, covered, for 50 to 60 minutes until physalis are tender but not broken up.

Strain physalis through a fine sieve, reserving solids and liquid separately. Measure 1 cup (250 mL) liquid, discarding remainder if any or adding more icewine if necessary. Pour 1/4 cup (50 mL) reserved liquid into a medium bowl; sprinkle gelatine over surface. Let stand for 5 minutes until puffy. Meanwhile, in a small saucepan, bring remaining liquid to a boil over high heat. Pour hot liquid over gelatine mixture, whisking constantly until gelatine has completely dissolved. Stir reserved cooked physalis into gelatine mixture. Ladle physalis mixture evenly into six 2/3 cup (150 mL) ramekins or 3/4 cup (175 mL) custard cups; refrigerate for at least 3 hours until firm. Cover with plastic wrap for longer storage.

To serve, remove jellies by running a small knife around edges then dipping base of ramekins briefly in hot water; unmold 1 jelly onto each of 6 plates. Unwrap foie gras. With a large, sharp knife, trim ends from foie gras; cut foie gras crosswise into 6 pieces, dipping knife in hot water between each cut. Place a piece of foie gras on each plate. Carefully peel back husks of physalis without removing them. Garnish each portion of foie gras with a physalis; garnish jellies with salad greens.
Makes 6 servings

Sweet little jellies raise the ambrosial pairing of foie gras and icewine to a whole new level. Physalis (also known as cape gooseberries or ground cherries) are golden bittersweet berries enclosed in a papery husk. Icewine vinegar is a unique Ontario product distilled from icewine and is available at specialty food stores.

PAN-SEARED PORK TENDERLOIN

with Braised Red Cabbage, Sweet & Sour Sauce & Brandied Apricots

Pork Tenderloin:
2 pork tenderloins (12 oz/375 g each)
12 dried apricots
1/3 cup (75 mL) brandy

Braised Red Cabbage:
2/3 cup (150 mL) red wine
1/2 cup (125 mL) red currant jelly
1/3 cup (75 mL) red wine vinegar
2 tbsp (25 mL) liquid honey
4 cups (1 L) shredded red cabbage
(about one-quarter of a large head)
1 Granny Smith apple, peeled, cored and thinly sliced
Half red onion, sliced
1 cinnamon stick, broken in half
5 dried juniper berries, crushed
1 bay leaf
1 tbsp (15 mL) olive oil
1 clove garlic, minced
Salt and pepper

Sweet & Sour Sauce:
1/4 cup (50 mL) red wine vinegar
1 tbsp (15 mL) red currant jelly
1/2 cup (125 mL) Veal Jus (page 217)
2 tbsp (25 mL) butter, softened
1 tsp (5 mL) lemon juice
Salt and pepper

To Finish:
1 tbsp (15 mL) butter
1 tsp (5 mL) olive oil
Salt and pepper
Salad greens

Pork Tenderloin: Trim off skinny ends of pork tenderloins (reserve trimmings for use in another recipe). With a small, sharp knife, trim off any silver skin from tenderloins by slipping the knife blade under it, angling blade slightly upward and cutting with a gentle back and forth motion. Wrap each tenderloin separately very tightly in plastic wrap, sealing ends well. Refrigerate for 24 hours. In a small bowl, combine apricots and brandy. Let stand, covered, at room temperature for 24 hours.

Braised Red Cabbage: In a large, non-reactive bowl, whisk together wine, red currant jelly, vinegar and honey; stir in red cabbage, apple, onion, cinnamon, juniper berries and bay leaf. Refrigerate, covered, for 24 hours.

In a large pot or Dutch oven, heat olive oil over medium heat. Add garlic; cook, stirring, for 30 seconds without browning. Add contents of bowl containing red cabbage; stir well. Bring to a boil over high heat; reduce heat to medium-low. Lay a piece of parchment paper directly over surface of cabbage; cover pot with a lid. Cook for 2 hours until cabbage is tender. Drain well. Season with salt and pepper to taste; keep warm.

Sweet & Sour Sauce: In a small saucepan, stir together vinegar and red currant jelly. Bring to a boil over medium-high heat, stirring to dissolve jelly. Cook, stirring, for 2 to 3 minutes until vinegar has evaporated, mixture is sticky and a spoon leaves a trail on bottom of saucepan. Stir in veal jus; bring to a boil. Boil, stirring often, for 3 minutes until reduced to 1/3 cup (75 mL) and sauce is thick enough to coat the back of a spoon. Remove from heat; gradually whisk in butter. Stir in lemon juice. Season with salt and pepper to taste. Keep warm but do not boil.

To Finish: Unwrap tenderloins; cut each crosswise into 6 even slices. In a large skillet, heat butter and oil over medium-high heat. Sprinkle pork medallions on both sides with salt and pepper; sear in batches for 4 minutes on each side until golden brown but still slightly pink in the middle, adding more butter and oil to skillet if necessary.

Divide red cabbage among 4 plates. Surround each portion with 3 pieces of pork. Drain apricots, discarding brandy; put 1 apricot on each piece of pork. Spoon over sauce, dividing evenly. Garnish with salad greens.
Makes 4 servings

Blanched kale and Brussels sprout leaves, sautéed in olive oil with a sprinkling of salt and pepper, are good with this. Wrapping the tenderloins tightly in plastic wrap before slicing helps to create uniformly round medallions of pork.

BAKED SEA BASS AGRUMES

with Citrus Essence, Celery Root Confit & Chervil Potatoes

Celery Root Confit:

One-quarter large celery root
1/2 cup (125 mL) Chicken Stock (page 217)
1 tbsp (15 mL) butter
1 tbsp (15 mL) olive oil
1 large sprig thyme
Salt and pepper
2 baby bok choy (8 oz/250 g),
halved lengthwise

Chervil Potatoes:

12 small fingerling potatoes (1 lb/500 g)
1 tbsp (15 mL) butter
1 tbsp (15 mL) chopped chervil
Salt and pepper

Sautéed Chanterelles:

1 tbsp (15 mL) olive oil
1 cup (250 mL) coarsely chopped
chanterelles (4 oz/125 g)
1 tsp (5 mL) finely chopped shallot
1/2 tsp (2 mL) minced garlic
1 tsp (5 mL) chopped parsley
Salt and pepper

Sea Bass Agrumes:

1 orange
1/3 cup (75 mL) butter
4 sea bass fillets (5 oz/150 g each)
1 tsp (5 mL) grated lemon rind
3 tbsp (45 mL) lemon juice
1 tbsp (15 mL) olive oil
1 tsp (5 mL) Tellicherry peppercorns, cracked
1 tsp (5 mL) pink peppercorns, cracked
1 cup (250 mL) Fish Stock (page 216)
1 tbsp (15 mL) white wine
Salt and pepper
Chervil
Lemon slices

Celery Root Confit: Peel celery root; cut into eight 1/4 inch (5 mm) slices. With a 2 inch (5 cm) cookie cutter, cut out 1 round from each slice, reserving trimmings for use in another recipe, such as stock. In a shallow, medium saucepan, combine celery root, chicken stock, butter, oil, thyme, and salt and pepper to taste; bring to a boil over high heat. Reduce heat to medium-low; simmer, uncovered, for 20 to 25 minutes until celery root is almost tender and liquid has reduced. Add bok choy to saucepan; cook, covered, for 6 to 8 minutes until bok choy is tender and wilted and cooking juices are syrupy. Toss gently to coat bok choy with cooking juices; keep warm.

Chervil Potatoes: In a steamer set over a saucepan of simmering water, steam potatoes for 15 to 20 minutes until tender. Remove from heat. When cool enough to handle, remove skin. Just before serving, melt butter in a medium saucepan. Add potatoes, chervil, and salt and pepper to taste; toss gently to heat through.

Sautéed Chanterelles: In a medium skillet, heat oil over medium-high heat. Add chanterelles; cook, stirring, for 3 to 5 minutes until golden and tender. Reduce heat to medium. Stir in shallot and garlic; cook, stirring often, for 2 to 3 minutes until shallot is softened but not brown. Stir in parsley, and salt and pepper to taste; keep warm.

Sea Bass Agrumes: Preheat the oven to 450°F (230°C). Grate 1/2 tsp (2 mL) rind from orange. Cut orange in half vertically through the stem. With a small, sharp knife, cut rind and white pith from one-half of orange; cut segments away from membrane. Coarsely chop segments; set aside. Squeeze juice from remaining half of orange; set aside.

Clarify 1/4 cup (50 mL) butter (see page 18); drizzle over base of a shallow baking dish large enough to hold the sea bass fillets in one layer. Lay sea bass fillets in dish. In a small bowl, whisk together orange and lemon rind, lemon juice, oil and peppercorns. Pour evenly over sea bass fillets; let stand for 10 minutes.

Pour fish stock, white wine and half of orange juice (reserve remainder) into dish; sprinkle sea bass lightly with salt. Cover dish tightly with foil; bake for 18 to 20 minutes until fish is firm to the touch. Remove fish to a warm platter, reserving cooking juices in dish. Remove skin from fish if you wish; keep fish warm.

Pour reserved cooking juices from fish into a medium saucepan; bring to a boil over medium-high heat. Boil for 10 to 12 minutes until reduced to 3/4 cup (175 mL). Remove from heat. Whisk in remaining butter until melted; stir in reserved orange segments and juice. Season with salt and pepper to taste.

Put 2 pieces of celery root in each of 4 shallow dishes, discarding thyme; top each portion with 3 potatoes. Spoon reduced orange sauce over potatoes. Arrange a piece of fish on top of potatoes; top with bok choy and chanterelles. Garnish with chervil and lemon slices.
Makes 4 servings

Named for a town on India's southwest coast, pungent Tellicherry black peppercorns are considered to be among the finest in the world, but if you can't find them, substitute regular black peppercorns.

WARM TART OF BLACK MISSION FIGS

& Goat Feta with Lavender Honey Drizzle

Half 397 g pkg frozen puff pastry, thawed

1/4 cup (50 mL) liquid honey

2 tsp (10 mL) dried lavender flowers

3 oz (75 g) firm goat feta

4 small ripe black mission figs,
each cut into 6 wedges

Salt

Salad:

1/4 cup (50 mL) olive oil

1 tbsp (15 mL) Champagne vinegar

Salt and pepper

2 cups (500 mL) lightly packed, washed
and dried arugula

2 cups (500 mL) lightly packed, washed
and dried frisée

1/4 cup (50 mL) chervil leaves

2 tbsp (25 mL) dill sprigs

4 sprigs lavender

4 sprigs chervil

Preheat the oven to 400°F (200°C). On a lightly floured surface, roll out puff pastry to 1/4 inch (5 mm) thickness. Using a saucer or small plate as a guide, cut out four 4 inch (10 cm) circles from pastry. Transfer to a large baking sheet; prick pastry circles all over with a fork. Lay a sheet of parchment paper over pastry circles; top with a second baking sheet. Bake for 10 to 12 minutes until golden brown and crisp. Remove top baking sheet and parchment; transfer pastry circles to a wire rack.

In a small heatproof bowl set over a saucepan of simmering water, warm honey for 2 minutes until it's runny enough to pour. Stir in lavender; leave over simmering water to infuse for 1 hour, checking occasionally to ensure water in saucepan doesn't evaporate. Strain honey through a small sieve, discarding lavender.

Preheat the oven to 400°F (200°C). Put pastry circles on a parchment-lined baking sheet. With a vegetable peeler or sharp knife, shave half of feta over pastry, dividing evenly. Arrange figs cut sides up in a circle on each tart. Crumble remaining feta; sprinkle over figs, dividing evenly. Drizzle a little lavender honey over each tart; sprinkle lightly with salt. Bake for 5 minutes until figs are warm and feta is just beginning to melt.

Salad: In a medium bowl, whisk together olive oil, vinegar and salt and pepper to taste. Add arugula, frisée, chervil and dill; toss well. Divide salad among 4 plates. Place a fig tart on each portion of salad. Drizzle tarts and edge of each plate with remaining honey. Garnish each tart with a sprig of lavender, and each salad with chervil.
Makes 4 servings

When plump mission figs are in season, these simple open-face tarts make a sweet little appetizer or light lunch.

Tresse of Sole & Salmon *(recipe on page 38)*

TRESSE OF SOLE & SALMON

with Champagne Sauce

Champagne Sauce:

2 cups (500 mL) Fish Stock (page 216)

1 cup (250 mL) sliced button mushrooms

(about 2 oz/50 g)

1/2 cup (125 mL) sliced shallots

1/2 cup (125 mL) white wine

1/2 cup (125 mL) Champagne

1 sprig thyme

1 cup (250 mL) whipping cream

2 tbsp (25 mL) butter, cubed

1 tsp (5 mL) lemon juice

Salt and pepper

Tresse:

Softened butter

4 skinless, boneless Dover sole fillets

(2-1/2 oz/65 g each)

9 x 1-1/2 inch (23 x 4 cm) piece boneless,

skinless Atlantic salmon fillet cut from the belly

(about 5 oz/150 g)

Champagne Sauce: In a wide, medium saucepan, stir together fish stock, mushrooms, shallots, white wine, 1/4 cup (50 mL) Champagne, and thyme; bring to a boil over high heat. Reduce heat to medium; boil for 1 hour, 15 minutes until liquid has reduced to 1 tbsp (15 mL) and is syrupy. Stir in remaining Champagne; boil for 3 minutes until liquid has reduced to 3 tbsp (45 mL). Stir in cream; bring to a boil over medium-high heat. Reduce heat to medium; boil for 5 minutes until liquid has reduced to 2/3 cup (150 mL) and sauce is thick enough to coat the back of a spoon. Remove from heat; gradually stir in butter until melted. Stir in lemon juice. Strain through a fine sieve into a clean saucepan. Season with salt and pepper to taste; set aside.

Tresse: Butter the outsides of four 1-1/2 inch (4 cm) diameter molds or shot glasses; have ready 4 toothpicks. Leaving 1 inch (2.5 cm) at the narrower tail end intact, cut each Dover sole fillet in half lengthwise. Trim salmon to an even thickness; cut lengthwise into 4 even strips. Put 1 Dover sole fillet on work surface with tail end away from you; carefully splay out the 2 halves without splitting it completely. Lining up one end of the salmon strip with the tail end of the sole fillet, lay a strip of salmon down centre of sole. Carefully weave the pieces of fish together as if you were making a braid without braiding them too tightly. Wrap the braided fish around the out-side of 1 mold; secure with a toothpick. Transfer fish-wrapped mold to a large plate. Repeat with remaining fish and molds; refrigerate until ready to serve.

Vegetable & Seafood Garnish: With a 1/2 inch (1 cm) melon baller, scoop 12 balls each from carrots (cutting 6 from each carrot), green and yellow zucchini and rutabaga. In a small saucepan of boiling salted water, cook rutabaga balls for 6 minutes, carrot balls for 4 minutes and zucchini balls for 2 minutes just until tender-crisp; drain well. Refrigerate until ready to serve. Trim ends of asparagus so each stalk is 4 inches (10 cm) long. With a vegetable peeler, peel skin from stem ends of asparagus. In a large skillet of boiling salted water, cook asparagus for 3 to 5 minutes until just tender. Drain well; refrigerate until ready to serve.

Scrub mussels under cold running water, snipping off beards with scissors if necessary and discarding any mussels that don't close when tapped sharply on the counter.

In a medium saucepan, heat oil over medium-high heat. Add mussels and wine; bring to a boil. Cover tightly; cook for 5 minutes or until mussels have opened. Strain through a colander, reserving cooking liquid. Remove mussels from shells, discarding shells. Refrigerate mussels and their cooking liquid until ready to serve.

Vegetable & Seafood Garnish:

2 large thick carrots

1 large green zucchini

1 large yellow zucchini

Half medium rutabaga

24 stalks asparagus

8 mussels

1 tbsp (15 mL) olive oil

1/2 cup (125 mL) white wine

4 oysters

1 tbsp (15 mL) butter

Salt and pepper

4 sea scallops

Chives

Scrub oysters well, paying attention to the hinge end where sediment can collect. Wearing a thick oven mitt, hold an oyster on work surface flat shell up; push the tip of an oyster knife into the hinge. With gentle force, press down diagonally, twisting the knife slightly to pry shells apart. Slide knife between shells, cutting oyster from top shell. Remove and discard top shell. Slide knife under oyster to release it from bottom shell; tip oyster and its juices into a small bowl. Repeat with remaining oysters. Cover and refrigerate oyster meat; discard shells.

To serve, use an egg lifter to carefully transfer fish-wrapped molds to a steamer set over a large skillet of boiling water; steam, covered, for 4 to 6 minutes until fish is opaque and firm. Meanwhile, in a medium skillet, heat butter over medium heat. Toss vegetable balls and asparagus in butter until heated through; season with salt and pepper to taste.

In a medium saucepan, stir together mussel cooking liquid and oyster juices; heat over medium-high heat until simmering. Sprinkle scallops on both sides with salt and pepper; add to saucepan. Reduce heat to medium; cook for 1 minute. Add mussels and oysters; cook for 1 to 2 minutes until scallops are opaque and mussels and oysters are hot. Reheat Champagne sauce over medium heat but do not boil.

With an egg lifter, carefully place 1 fish-wrapped mold in centre of each of 4 plates. Remove toothpicks; carefully slide out molds. Stand asparagus upright in each tresse, dividing evenly. Drain seafood; fill centre of each tresse with seafood. Spoon sauce over each tresse, dividing evenly; garnish each plate with vegetable balls and chives.
Makes 4 servings

Choose Atlantic salmon — it's less fragile and easier to work with than the Pacific variety — for this pretty presentation, which braids together 2 types of fish. I like to use strips cut from the belly side of the salmon fillet, as this part of the fish is fattier and is a good contrast to the lean sole. If you can't talk your fishmonger into selling you a piece from the belly, buy a fillet that weighs about 1-3/4 lb (875 g) and approximately 9 inches (23 cm) long. Cut the strips of fish you'll need for the tresse and use the rest of the fillet in another recipe.

HICKORY-SMOKED EEL

with Warm Potato Salad & Mustard Sauce

Hickory-Smoked Eel:

1 bottle (750 mL) red wine

2 stalks celery, coarsely chopped

1 onion, coarsely chopped

4 cloves garlic, crushed

1 tsp (5 mL) black peppercorns, cracked

1 large sprig thyme

1 bay leaf

4 pieces cleaned skinned eel (6 oz/175 g each)

4 cups (1 L) hickory wood chips

Chive Oil:

1 bunch chives (1/2 oz/15 g)

1/2 cup (125 mL) olive oil

Half clove garlic, sliced

Salt and pepper

Pancetta Chips:

4 thin slices pancetta (about 1-1/2 oz/40 g)

Mustard Sauce:

1 tbsp (15 mL) butter

2 tbsp (25 mL) chopped shallots

1 clove garlic, minced

1/4 cup (50 mL) white wine

3 button mushrooms, chopped

1 sprig thyme

1 bay leaf

1 cup (250 mL) Fish Stock (page 216)

1 cup (250 mL) whipping cream

1 tbsp (15 mL) grainy Dijon mustard

1 tsp (5 mL) lemon juice

Salt and pepper

Hickory-Smoked Eel: In a large, non-reactive bowl, stir together red wine, celery, onion, garlic, peppercorns, thyme and bay leaf. Add eel, ensuring pieces are completely submerged. Refrigerate, covered, for 24 hours.

Remove eel from marinade, discarding marinade. Using a smoker and following manufacturer's instructions, smoke eel over hickory chips until eel is tender and flakes easily. Alternatively, soak wood chips in a bowl of cold water for 30 minutes. Adjust oven rack to its lowest position and put a pizza stone on oven rack; preheat oven to 500°F (260°C). Spread hickory chips out on a rimmed, heavy baking sheet. Set an oiled rack on baking sheet; arrange eel in single layer on rack. Cover eel with a sheet of foil, oiling foil where it touches eel and crimping foil well around edges of baking sheet to seal completely. Place baking sheet directly on pizza stone; cook for 30 minutes. Reduce temperature to 250°F (120°C); cook for 2 hours until eel is tender and flakes easily. Remove from oven; let eel cool to room temperature, then refrigerate, covered, for 24 hours (this will make the texture of the eel firmer).

Chive Oil: In a small saucepan of boiling water, blanch chives for 30 seconds. With a slotted spoon, remove chives to a bowl of cold water. Drain well; wrap in paper towels and squeeze out excess moisture. Chop chives finely. In a blender (not a food processor), combine chives, oil, garlic and salt and pepper to taste; blend until finely minced. Strain through a fine sieve into a small bowl. (After serving, any remaining oil can be refrigerated, covered, for up to 3 days; use in salad dressings or for basting poultry or fish.)

Pancetta Chips: Preheat the oven to 400°F (200°C). Arrange pancetta in a single layer on a parchment-paper-lined baking sheet. Top with a second piece of parchment paper; set a second baking sheet on top of pancetta. Bake for 10 to 12 minutes until pancetta is crisp. Drain on a paper-towel-lined plate.

Mustard Sauce: In a medium saucepan, melt butter over medium heat. Add shallots and garlic; cook, stirring, for 3 to 5 minutes until softened but not browned. Add wine, mushrooms, thyme and bay leaf; bring to a boil over medium-high heat. Reduce heat to medium; boil for 3 to 5 minutes until liquid has reduced to 1 tbsp (15 mL). Add fish stock; bring to a boil over high heat. Reduce heat to medium-high; boil for 10 to 12 minutes until liquid has reduced to 1/3 cup (75 mL).

Stir in cream; bring to a boil over high heat. Reduce heat to medium-low; simmer for 12 to 15 minutes until liquid has reduced to 3/4 cup (175 mL) and sauce is thick enough to coat the back of a spoon. Strain through a fine sieve, discarding solids in sieve. Return to rinsed-out saucepan; whisk in mustard and lemon juice. Season with salt and pepper to taste; keep warm but do not boil.

Warm Potato Salad:

1 lb (500 g) small white waxy potatoes
1/3 cup (75 mL) Crème Fraîche (page 217)
2 green onions, finely chopped
2 tsp (10 mL) chopped chives
2 tsp (10 mL) chopped dill
2 tsp (10 mL) chopped parsley
1/2 tsp (2 mL) grated lemon rind
Salt and pepper

Garnish:

2 tbsp (25 mL) olive oil
2 tsp (10 mL) Champagne vinegar
Salt and pepper
2 cups (500 mL) lightly packed, washed and dried
baby salad greens (frisée, pea shoots,
chard and/or watercress)
2 tbsp (25 mL) chervil leaves
2 tsp (10 mL) chopped chives
2 tsp (10 mL) dill sprigs
Fennel fronds

Warm Potato Salad: In a steamer set over a saucepan of simmering water, steam potatoes for 20 to 25 minutes until just tender, being careful not to overcook. Remove from the heat. When potatoes are just cool enough to handle, remove skins; cut potatoes into 1/2 inch (1 cm) pieces. Return potatoes to steamer; cover and keep warm until ready to serve.

Meanwhile, in a medium bowl, stir together crème fraîche, green onions, chives, dill, parsley and lemon rind; set aside until ready to serve.

Garnish: In a small bowl, whisk together olive oil, vinegar and salt and pepper to taste. Just before serving, add greens, chervil, chives and dill; toss well.

To serve, preheat the oven to 300°F (150°C). With a butter knife, carefully scrape brown curd from outside of pieces of eel. With your fingers, carefully remove eel from bones in 3 or 4 pieces; arrange in single layer in a shallow ovenproof dish. Bake, covered, for 10 to 15 minutes, until hot.

Meanwhile, add potatoes to crème fraîche mixture; stir gently. Season with salt and pepper to taste. Set a metal ring or cookie cutter on 1 of 4 plates; spoon one-quarter of potato salad into ring, gently pressing on salad to hold it together. Gently push salad onto plate; remove ring. Repeat with remaining potato salad and plates. Insert the edge of 1 pancetta chip toward the back of each portion of potato salad; top potato salad with salad greens. Divide pieces of eel among plates. With an immersion blender, froth mustard sauce until foamy; spoon over eel. Decorate plates with drizzles of chive oil; garnish with fennel fronds.
Makes 4 servings

Most fish stores that carry eel sell them live but, if asked, will kill, skin and clean them for you. You'll need four 6 oz (175 g) pieces of eel for this recipe but any remaining eel can be frozen for use in a fish soup or bouillabaisse.

ROBBIE BURNS NIGHT

"When you go forth to waken the echoes, in the ancient and favourite

amusement of your forefathers, may pleasure ever be of your party."[1]

Be witness to the gathering of the Scottish clans, the legacy of an

ancient culture. Feel the thrill of the great Highland bagpipes and

drums. I can imagine the eerie lament of the lone piper in the hills.

Observe the ritual of piping in the haggis, held high, following the old

tradition. Be fascinated by the address to the haggis.

"His knife see rustic labour dight, And cut you up wi' ready slight,

Trenching your gushing entrails bright Like ony ditch; And then, oh,

what a glorious sight, Warm-reekin', rich!"[2]

I am elated to be part of this evening as I watch a gathering of friends,

sharing in the haggis, cock-a-leekie soup and trifle for the finish. A true

Scottish bill o' fare.

Robert Burns,[1] *Edinburgh, April 4, 1787* [2] *Mauchline, Scotland, 1813*

COCK-A-LEEKIE SOUP

8 cups (2 L) Chicken Stock (page 217)
1 skinless, boneless chicken breast
(about 6 oz/175 g)
6 pitted prunes
2 medium red-skinned potatoes
(12 oz/375 g), scrubbed
Salt
1 small leek (white and light green parts only)
2 tsp (10 mL) cornstarch
Vegetable oil for deep frying
Pepper
1 tbsp (15 mL) chopped parsley
1 tbsp (15 mL) chopped chives

In a medium saucepan, bring 2 cups (500 mL) of chicken stock to a simmer over medium-high heat. Add chicken breast. Reduce heat to medium-low; simmer, covered, for 15 to 20 minutes, turning once, until chicken is no longer pink inside. Remove chicken from saucepan (discard stock or reserve for use in another recipe). When cool enough to handle, cut chicken into thin 1 inch (2.5 cm) strips; set aside. Cut prunes into thin strips; set aside with chicken.

With a 1/2 inch (1 cm) melon baller, scoop about 24 balls from potatoes, dropping balls into a small saucepan of salted water as you work (alternatively, cut potatoes into 1/2 inch/1 cm cubes). Bring to a boil over high heat. Reduce heat to medium-low; cook, covered, for 5 minutes until almost tender when pierced with a slim knife. Drain well.

Wash leek well and drain; cut into thin 1 inch (2.5 cm) strips. Set aside half of the strips; pat remaining strips very dry on paper towels. In a small bowl, toss together dried leek strips and cornstarch until well combined.

In a deep-fat fryer and following manufacturer's instructions, heat vegetable oil to 325°F (160°C). Alternatively, pour oil into a large, wide pot to a depth of 1 inch (2.5 cm); heat over medium-high heat until a candy thermometer registers 325°F (160°C). If using a pot, reduce heat as necessary to maintain correct temperature.

Cook cornstarch-dusted leek in hot oil for about 30 seconds, stirring occasionally, until leek is golden and crisp. Remove with a slotted spoon; drain on a paper-towel-lined plate.

In a medium saucepan, combine remaining stock, potato balls and raw leek. Bring to a boil over high heat. Reduce heat to medium; simmer gently for 3 to 5 minutes until potato balls and leek are just tender. Season with salt and pepper to taste.

Divide chicken and prunes among 6 warm soup bowls; ladle chicken stock, potato balls and leek into soup bowls, dividing evenly. Sprinkle each serving with parsley, chives and deep-fried leek.
Makes 6 servings

This traditional Scottish soup of chicken and leeks is a mainstay on the menu of the Granite Club's annual Burns Supper, a celebration marking the birthday, on January 25, of renowned 18th century Scottish poet Robert Burns. The soup includes what may seem an unusual ingredient but the prunes add a terrific depth of flavour and slight sweetness to the broth.

CELEBRATION TRIFLE

Jelly Roll:

1/2 cup (125 mL) flour

1/2 tsp (2 mL) baking powder

Pinch table salt

3 eggs

1/2 cup (125 mL) sugar

1/2 tsp (2 mL) vanilla

1/2 cup (125 mL) raspberry jam

Egg Custard & Jelly:

4 egg yolks

2 cups (500 mL) milk

1/3 cup (75 mL) sugar

3 tbsp (45 mL) cornstarch

1 vanilla bean

1 tbsp (15 mL) butter

1 pkg (85 g) strawberry or raspberry

jelly powder

To Assemble:

2 ripe peaches, peeled, pitted and thinly sliced

2 ripe pears, peeled, cored and thinly sliced

1 cup (250 mL) whipping cream

1/4 cup (50 mL) icing sugar

Fresh berries and/or chocolate shavings

Jelly Roll: Preheat the oven to 350°F (180°C). Butter base and sides of a 15 x 10 inch (38 x 25 cm) jelly roll pan or rimmed baking sheet; line base with parchment paper.

Sift flour, baking powder and salt into a small bowl. In a medium bowl and using an electric mixer, beat eggs, sugar and vanilla for 5 minutes until thick and pale. Gently fold flour mixture into egg mixture until well combined. Gently pour batter into prepared pan, smoothing evenly and spreading to fill corners. Bake for 8 to 10 minutes until cake is golden and pulling away from sides of pan.

Loosen sides of cake; invert pan onto a large sheet of parchment paper. Remove pan from cake; peel off and discard parchment from base of cake. Starting from a short end, carefully roll up cake and parchment together; set aside on wire rack to cool completely. Unroll cooled cake; spread evenly with jam. Re-roll without parchment; set aside.

Egg Custard & Jelly: In a medium bowl, beat egg yolks. In a small saucepan, whisk together milk, sugar and cornstarch until smooth. Bring to a boil over medium-high heat, whisking constantly. Whisk about one-third of milk mixture into egg yolks; return yolk mixture to saucepan. Cook over medium-low heat, whisking constantly, for 3 to 5 minutes until custard is thickened and smooth (do not boil). Remove from heat; strain through a fine sieve into a medium bowl.

With a small knife, split vanilla bean lengthwise; scrape seeds from bean. Whisk vanilla seeds and butter into custard until butter melts. Let cool to room temperature; whisk well until smooth. Lay a piece of plastic wrap directly on surface of custard; refrigerate for 1-1/2 hours until chilled.

Prepare jelly powder according to instructions on the package. Refrigerate for 1-1/2 hours until jelly has thickened and is syrupy but not completely set.

To Assemble: Trim and discard crusty ends from jelly roll; cut jelly roll in half crosswise. Reserving one-half to serve at another meal, cut remaining jelly roll in half crosswise into 6 slices. Put 1 slice in base of each of six 2 cup (500 mL) individual dessert or wine glasses. Spoon peaches and pears over jelly roll, dividing evenly. Spoon about 1/3 cup (75 mL) custard into each glass, covering fruit completely and spreading right to edges of glass so there are no gaps. Carefully spoon about 1/3 cup (75 mL) jelly over each portion of custard. Chill for at least 2 hours until jelly has set.

Just before serving, in a medium bowl, whip cream and icing sugar until soft peaks form. Spoon whipped cream over each trifle, dividing evenly; garnish with berries and/or chocolate shavings.
Makes 6 servings

While fresh peaches and pears give the fullest flavour to this traditional layered dessert, if no ripe fruit is available, substitute one 14 oz (398 mL) can each of sliced peaches and pears, drained well before using.

GUEST CHEFS

The French preside over a great culinary heritage. Haute Cuisine, "classic cooking," was developed by the chefs of the French aristocracy and reached its pinnacle in the nineteenth century under the legendary French chef Auguste Escoffier. In the twentieth century the addition of Nouvelle Cuisine, "new cooking," broadened the culinary tradition by creating lighter dishes. Some of these new ideas were eventually woven among the classical and traditional threads of the great French culinary tapestry. The continuation of the line is so important. Guest chef Michel Bourdin, French chef of The Connaught for over 25 years, is a true ambassador of Escoffier. This master chef teaches the standard of perfection, sharing insights and expertise, inspiring the finest work from his protégés. For me, it was serendipity to be instructed by Bourdin in my early, impressionable years. He is my culinary mentor. Guest chefs provide members the opportunity to experience traditional Haute Cuisine prepared with the personal twist and style of the visiting chef.

WINTER GREENS

with Truffled Artichoke Mousse & Root Chips

Root Chips:

6 oz (175 g) root vegetables
(see note below)
Vegetable oil for deep frying
Salt

Truffled Artichoke Mousse:

1 lemon, cut into 8 wedges
4 large artichokes (8 oz/250 g each)
1-1/2 tsp (7 mL) sherry vinegar
1 tsp (5 mL) truffle oil
1/2 cup (125 mL) whipping cream
Salt and pepper

Winter Greens:

1 tbsp (15 mL) finely chopped shallot
1 tbsp (15 mL) sherry vinegar
1 tsp (5 mL) finely chopped black truffle
2 tbsp (25 mL) olive oil
1 tbsp (15 mL) truffle oil
6 cups (1.5 L) lightly packed, washed, dried
and torn winter greens (e.g., baby spinach,
radicchio, watercress and/or Belgian endive)
Chervil sprigs

Root Chips: Peel all vegetables. Using a mandolin slicer, very thinly slice vegetables, cutting carrots on the diagonal; pat very dry on paper towels, keeping varieties of vegetables separate. In a deep-fat fryer and following manufacturer's instructions, heat vegetable oil to 350°F (180°C). Alternatively, pour oil into a large, wide pot to a depth of 2 inches (5 cm); heat over medium-high heat until a candy thermometer registers 350°F (180°C). If using a pot, reduce heat as necessary to maintain correct temperature.

Working with 1 type of vegetable at a time, cook carrot in oil for 1 minute, beet and celery root for 1-1/2 to 2 minutes, and potato for 2 minutes, until crisp. Remove each batch with a slotted spoon; drain on a paper-towel-lined baking sheet. Season with salt to taste.

Truffled Artichoke Mousse: Put 4 lemon wedges in a large saucepan of cold water. Working with 1 artichoke at a time and being careful of the prickles, snap off all the leaves until a soft cone of inner leaves is revealed. Slice off cone with a sharp knife. Trim end of stem; cut artichoke in half lengthwise and peel stem. Using a teaspoon, scrape out the pointy thistles from the centre. Immediately rub artichoke all over with remaining lemon wedge, coating it well with juice to prevent browning. Drop artichoke and lemon wedge into saucepan. Repeat with remaining artichokes and lemon wedges.

Bring saucepan of artichokes to a boil over high heat. Reduce heat to medium-low; simmer, covered, for 15 minutes until tender. Drain well, discarding lemon wedges. In a food processor, pulse artichokes until a chunky purée forms, scraping down sides of processor once or twice. Rub purée through a fine sieve into a medium bowl, discarding solids in sieve. Stir in vinegar and truffle oil.

In a small bowl, whip cream until soft peaks form. Blend one-quarter of cream into artichoke mixture to lighten it, then gradually fold in remaining cream until no white streaks remain. Season with salt and pepper to taste.

Winter Greens: In a large bowl, whisk together shallot, vinegar and truffle; gradually whisk in olive and truffle oils until creamy. Season with salt and pepper to taste. Add greens; toss well.

Divide artichoke mousse among 4 plates, spooning into a circle in centre of each. Top mousse with greens, dividing evenly; tuck root chips in among greens. Garnish with chervil sprigs.
Makes 4 servings

Reynald Donet of Hôtellerie Beau Rivage in Condrieu, France, guest chef at the club in 2004, created this dramatic salad. Use a selection of root vegetables (celery root, beets, blue or regular potatoes, and orange, red or yellow carrots are all good choices) to make the crispy garnish and for best results serve them the day they're fried. Alternatively, to save time, buy good-quality, lightly salted root chips; you'll need about 2 oz (50 g) for 4 people.

CLASSIC PEACH NELLIE MELBA

Vanilla Ice Cream:

4 egg yolks

1/2 cup (125 mL) sugar

1 vanilla bean

1-1/2 cups (375 mL) half and half cream (10%)

1/2 cup (125 mL) whipping cream

Caramel Cage:

Vegetable oil

1/2 cup (125 mL) sugar

Poached Peaches:

1 cup (250 mL) water

1 cup (250 mL) white wine

1 cup (250 mL) sugar

1 vanilla bean

4 firm, ripe white peaches, halved and pitted

Raspberry Sauce:

2 cups (500 mL) fresh raspberries or 1 cup (250 mL) thawed unsweetened frozen raspberries

5 tbsp (65 mL) icing sugar

Vanilla Ice Cream: In a medium bowl, beat egg yolks. Add sugar; beat for 2 minutes until thick and pale. With a small knife, split vanilla bean lengthwise; scrape seeds from bean. In a medium saucepan, combine vanilla bean and its seeds, the half and half, and whipping cream; bring to a simmer over medium heat. Whisk one-third of cream mixture into egg yolk mixture; return yolk mixture to saucepan. Cook over medium-low heat for 2 to 3 minutes, whisking constantly, until custard loses its raw egg taste (do not boil). Remove from heat; strain through a fine sieve into a medium bowl. Add vanilla bean back into custard. Let cool to room temperature; whisk well until smooth. Lay a piece of plastic wrap directly on surface of custard; refrigerate until chilled.

Discard vanilla bean; pour custard into an ice cream maker and churn according to manufacturer's instructions. Alternatively, pour custard into a shallow 6 cup (1.5 L) container (preferably metal); freeze, covered, for 2 to 3 hours until a 1 inch (2.5 cm) frozen border has formed around edge. Scrape ice cream into a food processor; pulse until smooth and creamy. Scrape back into container. Repeat freezing and processing step once more; freeze, covered, for at least 3 hours until firm.

Caramel Cage: Line a baking sheet with parchment paper. Generously oil the curved underside of a 3 inch (8 cm) diameter ladle. In a small saucepan, heat sugar over medium heat, stirring often, until melted and golden. Keep sugar syrup warm over low heat. Holding ladle over baking sheet, dip tines of a fork into syrup; drizzle strands of syrup back and forth over curved side of ladle to form a lattice pattern. Let cool for 1 to 2 minutes; carefully ease caramel cage from ladle. Let cool on baking sheet. Repeat with remaining syrup to make 4 cages in all, oiling ladle well before drizzling with syrup. Store in a cool, dry place but do not refrigerate.

Poached Peaches: In a wide, shallow saucepan, combine water, white wine, sugar and vanilla bean over medium heat, stirring until sugar has dissolved. Bring to a boil over high heat; reduce heat to medium-low. Add peaches; cover and simmer gently for 10 to 15 minutes, turning occasionally, until peaches are tender but still hold their shape. Remove from heat; let cool slightly. When cool enough to handle, peel peaches, reserving poaching liquid. Put peach halves in a shallow dish; pour poaching syrup over them. Refrigerate, covered.

Raspberry Sauce: If using fresh raspberries, stir together raspberries and sugar in a small saucepan over medium-low heat for 2 to 3 minutes until raspberries are soft and release their juices. In a food processor, pulse raspberries until smooth. Strain through a fine sieve into a small bowl, discarding solids in sieve. If sauce is too thick, stir in a little water. If using frozen raspberries, add only 2-1/2 tbsp (32 mL) icing sugar and omit the cooking process, pulsing raspberries and sugar in food processor before straining.

To serve, scoop vanilla ice cream into 4 shallow dessert dishes; arrange 2 peach halves on top of each portion of ice cream. Drizzle raspberry sauce over peaches; top each with a caramel cage.
Makes 4 servings

Done well — with fresh peaches and raspberries and from-scratch ice cream — this timeless dessert has no peer. And neither does maître chef Michel Bourdin, executive chef of London, England's prestigious Connaught Hotel for more than 25 years. Peach Nellie Melba was the dessert Bourdin chose as the finale to the dinner he created for his guest appearance at the Granite Club in April 2007. If you can't find perfectly ripe white peaches, substitute regular peaches or 8 good-quality, drained, canned white peach halves.

Sweetbread Terrine (recipe on page 65)

APRIL
MAY
JUNE

A tiny Johnny-Jump-Up in the garden. What a thrilling find among the

wet leaves and the last bits of snow. What a pretty delicacy for the

side of a plate — just one — so I'll leave it for now. With the robin's

song and all the new shoots, spring has awakened. It is early morning

and the forest beckons. Off with my fox terrier I will go, as we do every

spring, for a day of morel hunting in the woods. With luck, and a sharp

eye, we will arrive home with our basket full and ready to cook.

EASTER

Rebirth. A burst of colour. Spring flowers, a light heart and family all around. What could be more perfect than serving loved ones a sweetbread terrine, a dish that celebrates the arrival of spring, a time when morels and wild leeks peek through the leaves on the forest floor. On an occasion such as this, I like to serve Mimosas — sparkling wine with freshly squeezed orange juice. To me, the essence of spring. For the kids at the table, orange juice with a splash of sparkling water. Everyone is included.

SWEETBREAD TERRINE

with Wild Leeks, Spring Mushrooms & Rhubarb Coulis

Sweetbread Terrine:

1 lb (500 g) veal sweetbreads

4 cups (1 L) Veal Stock (page 216)

2 egg whites

1/2 cup (125 mL) port

24 wild leeks

Salt

1 tbsp (15 mL) butter

8 oz (250 g) wild mushrooms (such as morels
and/or chanterelles), cleaned and chopped

2 tbsp (25 mL) finely chopped shallots

Pepper

4 tsp (20 mL) unflavoured powdered gelatine

1 tsp (5 mL) finely chopped chervil

1 tsp (5 mL) finely chopped chives

1 tsp (5 mL) finely chopped parsley

Rhubarb Coulis:

1 tbsp (15 mL) butter

2 cups (500 mL) coarsely chopped rhubarb
(approximately 3 stalks, leaves removed)

1/4 cup (50 mL) red wine vinegar

3 tbsp (45 mL) liquid honey

2 tsp (10 mL) minced fresh ginger

1 tbsp (15 mL) olive oil

Sweetbread Terrine: Rinse sweetbreads under cold running water to remove any excess blood. Put sweetbreads in a large saucepan of cold water; bring to a boil over high heat. Reduce heat to medium; simmer for 1 minute. With a slotted spoon, remove sweetbreads to a colander set in the sink; run cold water over sweetbreads until they are cool enough to handle. Carefully peel off and discard as much membrane as possible. In rinsed-out saucepan, bring stock to a simmer over high heat. Add sweetbreads; reduce heat to medium-low. Simmer, uncovered, for 10 minutes, turning once if sweetbreads are not completely submerged, until just firm. With a slotted spoon, remove sweetbreads to a shallow dish; refrigerate, reserving stock in saucepan.

In a small bowl, whisk egg whites until frothy. Add egg whites and port to stock; bring to a gentle boil over medium-high heat, stirring constantly, until egg whites form a raft. Reduce heat to medium-low; simmer, uncovered, for 15 minutes. Strain through a fine sieve lined with a double layer of cheesecloth. Rinse sieve well; line with a double layer of paper towel. Strain stock through paper-towel-lined sieve; let cool completely.

Wash leeks carefully under cold running water to remove any sand; trim root ends and just enough from leafy end so that leeks fit lengthwise in a 6 cup (1.5 L) terrine or loaf pan. Plunge leeks into a large pot or Dutch oven of boiling, salted water; bring back to a boil. Blanch leeks for 30 seconds; remove and drain on a clean towel. In a large skillet, heat butter over medium heat. Add mushrooms and shallots; cook, stirring often, for 5 to 7 minutes until mushrooms are golden and tender. Season with salt and pepper to taste; set aside to cool.

Measure 2 cups (500 mL) reserved stock (use remainder in another recipe). Pour 1/3 cup (75 mL) stock into a medium bowl; sprinkle gelatine over surface. Let stand for 5 minutes until puffy. Meanwhile, in a small saucepan, bring remaining stock to a boil over high heat. Pour hot stock over gelatine mixture, whisking constantly until gelatine has completely dissolved. In a small bowl, stir together chervil, chives and parsley. With a large, sharp knife, cut sweetbreads horizontally into 1/3 inch (8 mm) slices.

Pour 1/3 cup (75 mL) stock over base of a 6 cup (1.5 L) terrine or loaf pan. Arrange 8 leeks on top, alternating them top to tail; sprinkle lightly with herbs and salt and pepper. Top leeks with half of sweetbreads; sprinkle lightly with herbs and salt and pepper. Top sweetbreads with half of mushrooms; sprinkle lightly with herbs and salt and pepper. Pour over 1/3 cup (75 mL) stock. Repeat layers, ending with a layer of leeks, and pour remaining stock evenly over top. Refrigerate, covered, for 24 hours.

Rhubarb Coulis: In a medium saucepan, melt butter over medium heat. Add rhubarb; cook, stirring often, for 3 minutes or until rhubarb starts to soften. Stir in vinegar, honey and ginger; bring to a boil over medium-high heat. Reduce heat to medium-low; cook, stirring occasionally, for 2 to 4 minutes until rhubarb is tender and starting to break up; cool slightly. In a blender (not a food processor), blend rhubarb mixture and olive oil until smooth. Rub through a fine sieve into a small bowl; season with salt and pepper to taste. Let cool completely.

To serve, run a knife around inside edge of terrine pan; dip base of pan in hot water for a few seconds. Invert onto a cutting board. Cut terrine crosswise into slices; garnish with rhubarb coulis.
Makes 8 to 10 servings

Wild leeks, also called ramps, are in season for a short time in the spring. They resemble green onions but with broader leaves, and have a pronounced garlicky-onion flavour.

LAMB LOIN CHATELAINE

Lamb Jus:

2 large lamb racks (1 lb/500 g each)

1 carrot, coarsely chopped

1 stalk celery, coarsely chopped

2 tbsp (25 mL) coarsely chopped shallots

2/3 cup (150 mL) white wine

2 cups (500 mL) water

1 tbsp (15 mL) tomato paste

2 sprigs rosemary

2 bay leaves

1 sprig thyme

1/2 tsp (2 mL) black peppercorns

Salt and pepper

Mushroom Duxelle:

2 tbsp (25 mL) olive oil

1 lb (500 g) button mushrooms, quartered

2 tbsp (25 mL) chopped shallots

2 tsp (10 mL) minced garlic

3 tbsp (45 mL) whipping cream

Salt and pepper

Potato Galettes:

6 oz (175 g) mini (1 inch/2.5 cm) Yukon gold potatoes (about 6)

1/4 cup (50 mL) butter, clarified (page 18)

Salt and pepper

Lamb Jus: To bone lamb, set rack bony side up on cutting board. With a small, sharp knife, cut narrow meaty loin from bones, cutting as close to bones as possible. Cut off all excess fat and silvery skin from loin; repeat with remaining lamb rack. Cover and refrigerate loins.

Preheat the oven to 400°F (200°C). Put bones, fat and trimmings in a shallow roasting pan, along with carrot, celery and shallots. Roast, uncovered, for 30 minutes, until bones and vegetables are starting to brown. With a slotted spoon, remove bones and vegetables to a large saucepan. Pour off and discard excess fat from roasting pan; add wine to roasting pan. Bring to a boil over high heat, stirring to scrape up any browned bits from bottom of pan. Pour wine into saucepan; add water. Bring to a boil over high heat. As liquid comes to a boil, with a small strainer or large spoon, skim off the scum that rises to the top. Add tomato paste, rosemary, bay leaves, thyme and peppercorns; reduce heat to medium-low; simmer, uncovered, for 1 hour.

Strain stock through a colander into a medium bowl; discard solids in colander. Let cool to room temperature; refrigerate, covered, overnight.

Remove and discard fat from surface of stock; spoon stock into a medium saucepan. Bring to a boil over high heat. Adjust heat so stock still boils but doesn't splatter; boil for 6 to 8 minutes until reduced to 2/3 cup (150 mL). Season with salt and pepper to taste. Refrigerate, covered, until ready to serve.

Mushroom Duxelle: In a large skillet, heat oil over medium-high heat. Add mushrooms; cook, stirring, for 5 to 7 minutes until golden and tender. Add shallots and garlic; cook, stirring often, for 3 to 5 minutes until shallots are softened but not brown. Spoon into a fine sieve set over a bowl; let cool completely. Discard any liquid in bowl.

In a food processor, pulse mushroom mixture until coarsely chopped. Return mushroom mixture to skillet; add cream. Cook, stirring, over medium heat for 2 to 3 minutes until heated through. Season with salt and pepper to taste; keep warm.

Potato Galettes: Peel potatoes. On a mandolin slicer or with a very sharp knife, slice potatoes into 1/16 inch (1.5 mm) slices. In a medium bowl, toss potatoes with clarified butter, and salt and pepper to taste. Set four 3 inch (8 cm) metal ring molds or cookie cutters in a medium, good-quality, non-stick skillet. Arrange potato slices in molds, dividing evenly and overlapping slices until no spaces remain. Put skillet over medium heat; cook for 4 to 6 minutes, without removing ring molds, until underside of galettes are golden brown. Remove ring molds; carefully turn galettes over; cook for 4 to 6 minutes until golden and potatoes are tender. Transfer galettes to a small baking sheet; set aside. (If you only have 1 ring mold or cookie cutter, prepare galettes individually, forming a second one once the first has been flipped.)

Lamb Loins:

1 tbsp (15 mL) vegetable oil

2 cups (500 mL) lightly packed spinach leaves (stems removed before measuring)

1 tsp (5 mL) dried herbes de Provence

Salt and pepper

2 oz (50 g) caul fat

Buttered Cabbage:

2 cups (500 mL) well-packed shredded Savoy cabbage (one-quarter of a head)

2 tbsp (25 mL) butter

Salt and pepper

Lamb Loins: In a medium skillet, heat oil over medium-high heat. Sear reserved lamb loins for 3 minutes or until browned on all sides. Remove lamb loins to a plate; let cool completely.

Meanwhile, wash spinach leaves in cold water; drain well. In a wide, shallow, covered saucepan over medium heat, cook spinach in the water clinging to it for 2 to 3 minutes until just wilted. Carefully remove spinach leaves from saucepan; spread out in a single layer on a clean towel to cool.

Preheat the oven to 400°F (200°C). Sprinkle lamb loins evenly with herbes de Provence, and salt and pepper to taste. Wrap each loin in spinach leaves, overlapping leaves to cover loins completely; wrap each tightly in caul fat, tucking in ends of caul fat. Put loins seam side down in a small, shallow roasting pan; roast for 15 minutes for medium-rare. Remove to a cutting board and cover loosely with foil; let rest for 5 minutes. Turn off oven; put baking sheet containing galettes in oven to warm. Reheat jus in small saucepan over medium heat.

Buttered Cabbage: In a medium saucepan of boiling salted water, blanch cabbage for 3 minutes until just tender. Drain well. In same saucepan, heat butter over medium heat; add cabbage and season with salt and pepper to taste; toss well. Keep warm.

To serve, slice each loin into 6 even-size pieces; divide among 4 plates. Set a 3 inch (8 cm) diameter metal ring or cookie cutter on one plate. Spoon one-quarter of cabbage into ring; top cabbage with one-quarter mushroom duxelle, gently pressing on ingredients to hold them together. Gently push vegetables onto plate; remove ring. Repeat with remaining cabbage, mushrooms and plates. Top each stack of vegetables with a potato galette; garnish with thyme. Spoon jus around lamb.

Makes 4 servings

Ask your butcher to bone the lamb racks, removing the loin from each and retaining all the bones (which you'll need for the sauce), or bone them yourself as described in the recipe. Caul fat is lacy membrane that lines a pig's abdominal cavity; it's used to add moisture to lean cuts of meat, and melts during cooking. If herbes de Provence are unavailable, substitute 1/4 tsp (1 mL) each chopped fresh thyme, rosemary and sage leaves.

MOTHER'S DAY

In honour of Mums and Grandmamas. What a wonderful reason to
set aside a special day. Showing our appreciation. Making it
memorable. Spending time together and sharing our table with
those we love. To mark the occasion, I have selected lighthearted
springtime recipes that are intriguing little conversation pieces. The
paillard of salmon "façon Troisgros" is a simple French dish originally
created and made famous by the Troisgros family in Roanne, France.
A special dish for a special person. For dessert, I have included one
of Mum's timeless favourites, Lemony Floating Islands. The children
in the family make little cupcakes with swirls of sugary icing, such
a treat, with scoops of pink strawberry ice cream in pretty little
dishes, just for Mum.

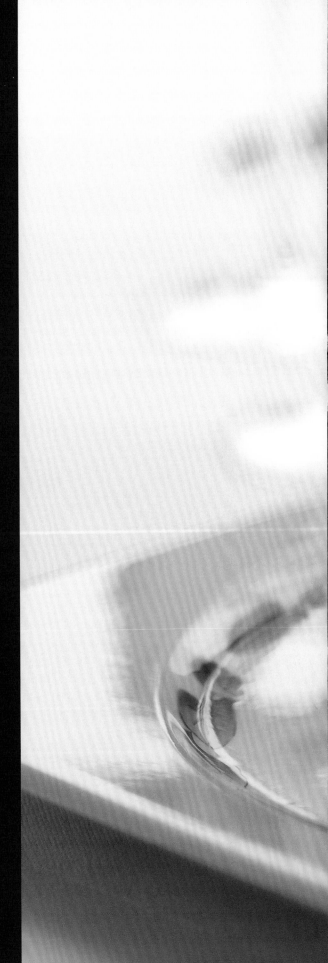

Camembert Phyllo Towers (recipe on page 76)

PAILLARD OF SALMON

façon Troisgros

24 stalks white asparagus

16 stalks green asparagus

2 tsp (10 mL) cornstarch

Vegetable oil for deep frying

1/2 cup (125 mL) Fish Stock (page 216)

1/3 cup (75 mL) Sancerre or other white wine

2 tbsp (25 mL) finely chopped shallots

1 tbsp (15 mL) Noilly Prat or other dry vermouth

1 cup (250 mL) whipping cream

2 cups (500 mL) lightly packed sorrel leaves
(tough stems removed before measuring),
finely shredded

1 tbsp (15 mL) lemon juice

3 tbsp (45 mL) butter

Salt and pepper

2 skinless centre-cut salmon fillets
(6 oz/175 g each)

Trim at least 1 inch (2.5 cm) from ends of asparagus, ensuring stalks are all the same length. With a vegetable peeler, peel skin from stem ends of asparagus, reserving peelings from green asparagus. Set asparagus aside. Pat peelings dry on paper towels. In a small bowl, toss together peelings and cornstarch until well combined.

In a deep-fat fryer and following manufacturer's instructions, heat vegetable oil to 325°F (160°C). Alternatively, pour oil into a large, wide pot to a depth of 1 inch (2.5 cm); heat over medium-high heat until a candy thermometer registers 325°F (160°C). If using a pot, reduce heat as necessary to maintain correct temperature.

Cook peelings in hot oil for about 30 seconds, stirring occasionally, until peelings are golden and crisp. Remove with a slotted spoon; drain on a paper-towel-lined plate.

In a small saucepan, stir together fish stock, Sancerre, shallots and Noilly Prat; bring to a boil over medium-high heat. Boil for 8 to 10 minutes until liquid has reduced to 1 tbsp (15 mL). Stir in cream; bring to a boil. Reduce heat to medium; boil for 8 to 10 minutes until sauce has reduced to 3/4 cup (175 mL) and is thick enough to coat the back of a spoon. Remove from heat; stir in sorrel and lemon juice. Whisk in 1 tbsp (15 mL) butter until melted; season with salt and pepper to taste. Keep warm but do not boil.

In a large skillet of boiling salted water, cook asparagus for 3 to 5 minutes until just tender. Drain well. With a slim, sharp knife, carefully cut each salmon fillet in half horizontally to make four 3 oz (75 g) pieces. Sprinkle on both sides with salt and pepper. In a large, good-quality, non-stick skillet, heat 1 tbsp (15 mL) butter over medium heat. Add salmon; cook for 1 to 2 minutes, turning once, until firm to the touch but still translucent in the centre. Meanwhile, in a medium skillet, heat remaining butter over medium heat. Toss asparagus in butter; season with salt and pepper to taste.

To serve, spoon sauce onto the centre of each of 4 plates. Place a piece of salmon in centre of each portion of sauce. Arrange 2 white stalks of asparagus on each portion of salmon; top with 2 green stalks at right angles to the white. Repeat stacking white and green asparagus, using 6 stalks of white asparagus and 4 of green for each portion. Pile deep-fried asparagus peelings on top of each stack, dividing evenly.
Makes 4 servings

This simple salmon preparation has been a signature dish for more than 45 years at the famed Hôtel Restaurant Troisgros in the French town of Roanne, where I was lucky enough to experience a year of my training. To achieve the neat squares of salmon needed for this recipe, you'll need two 6 oz (175 g) pieces of centre-cut salmon cut from the backbone side of the fillet. If you have a good relationship with your fishmonger he may cut these pieces for you. Otherwise, buy a 1-1/2 lb (750 g) piece of centre-cut fillet. When you get home, cut it in half lengthwise, reserving the belly portion for another use, then cut the remaining piece of salmon in half crosswise and follow the instructions in the recipe for cutting the paillards.

GOAT CHEESE BONBONS

with Oven-Dried Grapes & Pear-Cassis Reduction

Oven-Dried Grapes:

20 medium seedless red grapes

Pear-Cassis Reduction:

1 cup (250 mL) red wine

1/2 cup (125 mL) cassis (black currant liqueur)

1 ripe Anjou or Bartlett pear, peeled, cored and coarsely chopped

20 seedless red grapes

2 tbsp (25 mL) coarsely chopped shallots

1 tbsp (15 mL) coarsely chopped fresh ginger

10 black peppercorns

1 cinnamon stick, broken in half

3 sprigs thyme

2 whole cloves

1 bay leaf

Salt and pepper

Goat Cheese Bonbons:

3 oz (75 g) soft goat cheese

2 tsp (10 mL) finely chopped chives

2 tsp (10 mL) finely chopped parsley

Salt and pepper

4 sheets frozen phyllo pastry, thawed according to package directions

1/2 cup (75 mL) butter, clarified (page 18)

Oven-Dried Grapes: Preheat the oven to 250°F (120°C). Arrange grapes about 1 inch (2.5 cm) apart on a wire rack set on a baking sheet. Bake for 2 hours or until shrivelled but still moist, watching carefully toward the end of cooking time to ensure grapes don't scorch. Let cool completely. (Grapes can be refrigerated, tightly covered, for up to 2 days.)

Pear-Cassis Reduction: In a medium, non-reactive saucepan, combine red wine, cassis, pear, grapes, shallots, ginger, peppercorns, cinnamon stick, thyme, cloves and bay leaf; bring to a boil over high heat. Reduce heat to medium-low; simmer, uncovered, for 20 minutes until pear is tender. Let cool slightly; strain through a fine sieve, reserving solids and liquid separately. Discard cinnamon.

In a food processor, pulse solids until finely chopped. With motor running, add enough of the reserved liquid to make a mixture the consistency of applesauce. Strain mixture through a fine sieve; return to rinsed-out saucepan, discarding solids and any remaining liquid. Season with salt and pepper to taste; set aside.

Goat Cheese Bonbons: Line a baking sheet with parchment paper. In a small bowl, mash goat cheese to soften it slightly; mash in chives, parsley, and salt and pepper to taste until well combined. Divide goat cheese into 12 even-size pieces.

Lay a sheet of phyllo on work surface with a long end toward you; brush generously with clarified butter. Top with second sheet of phyllo; brush with more butter. Repeat with remaining phyllo and butter, making a stack of 4 sheets of phyllo. Cut phyllo into 12 even-size squares, making 3 vertical and 2 horizontal cuts. Working quickly, form a piece of goat cheese into a narrow log; centre on the edge of 1 piece of phyllo. Roll up phyllo to enclose goat cheese, pinching ends then twisting gently so package resembles a wrapped candy. Put seam side down on a baking sheet; repeat with remaining goat cheese and phyllo. Brush with remaining butter; refrigerate for at least 30 minutes. Preheat the oven to 400°F (200°C). Bake for 6 to 8 minutes or until golden brown and crisp.

To serve, reheat pear-cassis reduction; spoon a pool of reduction on each of 4 plates. Arrange 3 goat cheese bonbons on each plate; garnish with oven-dried grapes.

Makes 4 servings

It's worth investing in an oven thermometer as even the most efficient stove can be wildly inaccurate at a very low temperature, such as that needed for oven-drying the grapes for this pretty appetizer.

CAMEMBERT PHYLLO TOWERS

with Red Onion Marmalade

Red Onion Marmalade:
1/2 cup (125 mL) sugar
1/2 cup (125 mL) red wine
2 tbsp (25 mL) red wine vinegar
2 tbsp (25 mL) liquid honey
2 medium red onions, thinly sliced

Camembert Phyllo Towers:
2 tbsp (25 mL) pink peppercorns
1 tsp (5 mL) chopped chervil
8 sheets frozen phyllo pastry,
thawed according to package directions
1/2 cup (125 mL) butter, clarified (page 18)
6 oz (175 g) Camembert cheese,
cut into 4 even pieces
Pea shoots

Red Onion Marmalade: In a medium, non-reactive saucepan, stir together sugar, red wine, vinegar and honey; bring to a boil over medium-high heat. Add onions; reduce heat to medium-low. Simmer, covered, for 10 minutes until onions are soft. Uncover saucepan; increase heat to medium. Cook, stirring occasionally, for 25 to 30 minutes until liquid is reduced and syrupy and onion is very soft. Spoon onion marmalade into a sieve set over a bowl; let cool completely, reserving onion marmalade and drained juices separately.

Camembert Phyllo Towers: Line a baking sheet with parchment paper. With your fingers, rub peppercorns through a fine sieve so that the flaky outer husk comes off the peppercorns; you should have approximately 1 tsp (5 mL) husks. Reserving the peppercorns to put in your grinder, stir the outer husks and chervil together in a small bowl; set aside.

Lay a sheet of phyllo on work surface with a long end toward you; brush generously with clarified butter. Sprinkle with one-eighth of peppercorn-chervil mixture. Top with second sheet of phyllo; brush with more butter and sprinkle with more peppercorn-chervil mixture. Repeat to make a stack of 4 sheets of phyllo. Cut phyllo in half vertically to make 2 even-size pieces. Put a piece of cheese in centre of each piece of phyllo; gently gather phyllo up around cheese to enclose, so that excess phyllo stands vertically. Place on baking sheet.

Repeat process to make another stack of 4 sheets of phyllo and use to wrap remaining pieces of cheese. Refrigerate for at least 30 minutes or overnight. Preheat the oven to 350°F (180°C). Lay towers on their sides on baking sheet; bake for 20 to 25 minutes until pastry is golden brown and crisp.

Using a slotted spoon, spoon onion marmalade in centre of each of 4 plates, dividing evenly; top each portion with a phyllo tower, nestling it into marmalade so that it stands upright. Drizzle plates with some of the reserved cooking juices from marmalade. Garnish with pea shoots.
Makes 4 servings

There's no need to remove the rind from the Camembert for this sensational appetizer.

FLOATING ISLANDS

with Caramel Sauce

Spun Sugar:

3/4 cup (175 mL) sugar

Vegetable oil

Crème Anglaise:

6 egg yolks

1/2 cup (125 mL) sugar

1 vanilla bean

2 cups (500 mL) milk

Caramel Sauce:

3/4 cup (175 mL) whipping cream

1/3 cup (75 mL) sugar

1/4 cup (50 mL) glucose syrup

1 tbsp (15 mL) butter, softened

Floating Islands:

2 cups (500 mL) milk

2 cups (500 mL) water

4 egg whites

1/2 cup (125 mL) sugar

1 tsp (5 mL) vanilla

1/2 tsp (2 mL) cream of tartar

1/2 tsp (2 mL) grated lemon rind

Pistachios

Mint sprigs

Spun Sugar: Line a baking sheet with parchment paper. In a small saucepan, heat sugar over medium heat, stirring often, until melted and golden. Keep sugar syrup warm over low heat. Generously oil the handle of a wooden spoon. Holding spoon by its bowl over baking sheet, dip tines of a fork into syrup; rapidly flick strands of syrup back and forth over handle of spoon to form a "cloud" of spun sugar. Let cool for 1 to 2 minutes; carefully ease spun sugar from spoon. Let cool on baking sheet. Repeat with remaining syrup to make 6 clouds in all, oiling spoon well before drizzling with syrup. Store in a cool, dry place until ready to serve but do not refrigerate.

Crème Anglaise: In a medium bowl, beat egg yolks. Add sugar; beat for 2 minutes until thick and pale. With a small knife, split vanilla bean lengthwise; scrape seeds from bean. In a medium saucepan, combine vanilla bean and its seeds and the milk; bring to a simmer over medium heat. Whisk about one-third of milk into egg yolk mixture; return yolk mixture to saucepan. Cook over medium-low heat for 2 to 3 minutes, whisking constantly, until custard loses its raw egg taste (do not boil). Remove from heat; strain through a fine sieve into a medium bowl. Add vanilla bean back into custard. Let cool to room temperature; whisk well until smooth. Lay a piece of plastic wrap directly on surface of custard; refrigerate until chilled.

Caramel Sauce: In a small saucepan, bring cream to a boil over medium heat. Remove from heat; cover. Meanwhile, in a medium heavy-based saucepan, stir together sugar and glucose syrup over medium-high heat. Cook for 2 to 3 minutes, stirring constantly, until sugar has almost completely dissolved. Cook, without stirring, until caramel is a very pale gold. Reduce heat to medium; cook, without stirring, for 2 minutes until caramel is deep gold and a candy thermometer registers 350°F (180°C). Remove saucepan from heat; whisk in butter until melted (mixture may form clumps). Return saucepan to low heat; gradually whisk in cream, standing back in case mixture splatters. Continue to whisk until sauce is completely smooth and any lumps of caramel have melted. Remove from heat; let cool completely. Whisk well before serving.

Floating Islands: In a large, shallow saucepan, bring milk and water to a simmer over medium heat. Meanwhile, in a medium bowl, beat egg whites until soft peaks form. Add sugar, vanilla, cream of tartar and lemon rind; beat until stiff peaks form.

Line a large baking sheet with paper towels. With 2 dessert spoons, form an oval shape from egg white; drop gently into the simmering milk. Repeat until you've formed 4 ovals. Poach for 5 minutes, turning gently with clean spoons after 3 minutes. With a slotted spoon, remove poached egg whites from milk; place on prepared baking sheet. Repeat with remaining egg whites, poaching 4 ovals at a time, to make 16 in all.

To serve, spoon crème anglaise into 4 shallow bowls, dividing evenly. Carefully place 4 floating islands on each pool of crème anglaise. Drizzle tops of floating islands with caramel sauce; scatter with pistachios. Top each portion with spun sugar; garnish with mint.
Makes 4 servings

Known in France as oeufs à la neige *(snow eggs), this spectacular dessert makes a dramatic finale to any meal. Glucose syrup is thick, white corn syrup; look for it in your local bulk store.*

SUMMER DINING

The taste of food is a little different in the golden light of a late summer day, surrounded by the natural aromas of flowers and freshly cut grass. To me, there is no greater indulgence than whiling away a late afternoon in the comfort of a lawn chair, nibbling on appetizers, in anticipation of the main dish. The foods we crave are fresh, light and flavourful. How perfect Nouvelle Cuisine, "new cooking," is for this time of year! Lighter, but still based on classical French precepts. For the finish, the summer's best fruit with a big dollop of whipped cream or a sprinkle of sugar.

Seared Arctic Char (recipe on page 82)   79

SEARED ARCTIC CHAR

with Fennel Slaw & Smoked Tomato Sauce

Smoked Tomato Sauce:
4 plum tomatoes, quartered and cored
4 cups (1 L) hickory wood chips
1/2 tsp (2 mL) Dijon mustard
1/2 tsp (2 mL) Champagne vinegar
1/2 cup (125 mL) olive oil
Salt and pepper

Fennel Slaw:
Half bulb fennel
2 tbsp (25 mL) lemon juice
2 tbsp (25 mL) olive oil
1/2 tsp (2 mL) chopped thyme
Salt and pepper

Roasted Fingerlings:
8 large fingerling potatoes (1 lb 6 oz/675 g)
1 tbsp (15 mL) olive oil
Salt and pepper

Seared Arctic Char:
1 tbsp (15 mL) olive oil
4 Arctic char fillets with skin (6 oz/175 g each),
pin bones removed with tweezers
Salt and pepper
Wilted Spinach (page 203)
16 pieces Oven-Dried Plum Tomato (page 217)
Basil Oil (page 115)
Diced red and yellow tomato

Smoked Tomato Sauce: Using a smoker and following manufacturer's instructions, smoke tomatoes over hickory chips until tomatoes are tender but not broken up. Alternatively, soak wood chips in a bowl of cold water for 30 minutes. Adjust oven rack to its lowest position and put a pizza stone on oven rack; preheat oven to 500°F (260°C). Spread hickory chips out on a rimmed, heavy baking sheet. Set a rack on baking sheet; arrange tomatoes cut sides up in a single layer on rack.

Cover tomatoes with a sheet of foil, oiling foil where it touches tomatoes and crimping foil well around edges of baking sheet to seal completely. Place baking sheet directly on pizza stone; cook for 30 minutes. Reduce temperature to 250°F (120°C); cook for 30 minutes until tomatoes are tender but not broken up. Let cool slightly.

In a blender (not a food processor), blend tomatoes, mustard and vinegar until fairly smooth. With the motor running, gradually add olive oil through lid until sauce is smooth and creamy. Rub sauce through a fine sieve, discarding solids in sieve. Season with salt and pepper to taste; set aside.

Fennel Slaw: Trim feathery tops from fennel; reserve for garnish. Trim fennel and cut in half, removing tough core. With a mandolin slicer, cut fennel into wafer-thin slices. In a medium, non-reactive bowl, toss fennel with lemon juice, oil, thyme, and salt and pepper to taste. Let stand at room temperature for at least 15 minutes for flavours to blend.

Roasted Fingerlings: Preheat the oven to 400°F (200°C). In a medium saucepan of boiling salted water, cook potatoes for 10 minutes; drain well. Return saucepan to low heat; shake saucepan gently to dry potatoes. Cut potatoes in half lengthwise. On a large, rimmed baking sheet, toss potatoes with oil, and salt and pepper to taste. Roast for approximately 25 minutes, stirring occasionally, until potatoes are golden brown and tender. Keep warm.

Seared Arctic Char: Meanwhile, in a large skillet, heat oil over medium-high heat. Sprinkle Arctic char fillets on both sides with salt and pepper to taste. Add to fillets to skillet; cook for 2 to 4 minutes, turning once, until golden brown on both sides and just firm to the touch.

Divide fingerlings among 4 plates; top with spinach, dividing evenly. Arrange oven-dried tomatoes on top of spinach. Top each portion with an Arctic char fillet; spoon fennel slaw over fish. Drizzle plates with smoked tomato sauce and basil oil; garnish with reserved fennel tops and diced tomato.
Makes 4 servings

You'll have smoked tomato sauce left over after serving this wonderful fish dish but since it's sensational with grilled chicken, ribs or salmon, that's no hardship!

TIAN OF CAPRESE SALAD

Balsamic Glaze:

1/4 cup (50 mL) good-quality aged balsamic vinegar

1 tsp (5 mL) liquid honey

Caprese Salad:

3 balls buffalo mozzarella
(4 to 5 oz/125 to 150 g each), drained

3 medium tomatoes (see note below)

4 cherry tomatoes

1/4 cup (50 mL) olive oil

2 tbsp (25 mL) finely chopped basil

1 tbsp (15 mL) finely chopped shallot

Salt and pepper

Basil sprigs

Edible flowers

Balsamic Glaze: In a small saucepan, stir together balsamic vinegar and honey; bring to a boil over medium-high heat. Boil for 2 to 3 minutes until syrupy and reduced to 2 tbsp (25 mL). Remove from heat; let cool.

Caprese Salad: Cut each piece of mozzarella into 4 even-size slices, discarding ends; arrange in a single layer on a paper-towel-lined platter. Refrigerate until ready to serve.

Cut a small X in the bottom of each tomato. In a medium saucepan of boiling water, blanch medium tomatoes for 30 seconds and cherry tomatoes for 10 seconds. Remove with a slotted spoon and immediately immerse in a bowl of ice water. Remove from water; peel all skin from medium tomatoes. Carefully peel skin from cherry tomatoes without removing it completely so skin resembles petals of a flower, using a small, sharp knife to lengthen splits in skin if necessary; set aside.

Just before serving, remove paper towel from platter holding mozzarella. Drizzle mozzarella with 2 tbsp (25 mL) olive oil; sprinkle with 1 tbsp (15 mL) basil, 1-1/2 tsp (7 mL) shallot, and salt and pepper to taste. Cut each medium tomato crosswise into 4 slices, discarding ends; arrange slices in a single layer on a large plate. Drizzle with remaining olive oil; sprinkle with remaining basil, shallot, and salt and pepper to taste.

On each of 4 plates, stack tomato and mozzarella slices in alternate layers, starting with tomato and finishing with cheese. Drizzle each plate with balsamic glaze; garnish with cherry tomatoes, basil and edible flowers.
Makes 4 servings

For the prettiest presentation, use a red, a yellow and an orange tomato for this summery salad.

GRILLED CHICKEN BREAST

with Sweet Pea Emulsion & Wild Mushroom Risotto

Wild Mushroom Risotto:

1 tbsp (15 mL) butter

2 tbsp (25 mL) finely chopped shallots

1 cup (250 mL) arborio rice

1/4 cup (50 mL) white wine

1 bay leaf

1-1/4 cups (300 mL) hot Chicken Stock
(page 217)

Sweet Pea Emulsion:

20 sugar snap peas (4 oz/125 g)

2 tbsp (25 mL) butter

3 tbsp (45 mL) sliced shallots

1/4 cup (50 mL) white wine

1 sprig thyme

1 bay leaf

1/2 cup (125 mL) Chicken Stock (page 217)

3/4 cup (175 mL) whipping cream

1/4 cup (50 mL) frozen peas, thawed and drained

Salt and pepper

Grilled Chicken Breasts:

4 boneless chicken breasts with skin
(6 to 8 oz/175 to 250 g each)

Salt and pepper

To Finish:

2 tbsp (25 mL) butter

2 cups (500 mL) chopped
mushrooms (5 oz/150 g)

1 cup (250 mL) hot Chicken Stock (page 217)

1/3 cup (75 mL) grated Parmesan cheese

2 tbsp (25 mL) mascarpone cheese

1 tbsp (15 mL) chopped chives

Salt and pepper

2 slices bacon

Steamed snow peas

Pea shoots

Edible flowers

Wild Mushroom Risotto: In a medium saucepan, heat butter over medium heat. Add shallots; cook, stirring, for 3 to 5 minutes until softened but not brown. Add rice; stir until well coated with butter. Add wine and bay leaf; bring to a boil. Simmer for 1 to 2 minutes, stirring often, until wine has been absorbed. Add chicken stock, 1/4 cup (50 mL) at a time, stirring constantly and allowing each batch of stock to be absorbed by rice before adding the next one. Remove from heat; set aside. (Risotto won't be completely cooked.)

Sweet Pea Emulsion: Shell sugar snap peas, reserving peas and shells separately; coarsely chop shells. In a small saucepan, heat 1 tbsp (15 mL) butter over medium heat. Add shallots; cook, stirring, for 3 to 5 minutes until softened but not brown. Add wine, thyme and bay leaf; bring to a boil over medium-high heat. Boil for 2 to 3 minutes until liquid is reduced to 2 tbsp (25 mL). Add chicken stock; bring to a boil. Boil for 5 to 7 minutes until liquid is reduced to 1/4 cup (50 mL). Add cream; bring to a boil. Reduce heat to medium; boil for 8 minutes or until sauce has reduced to 3/4 cup (175 mL) and is thick enough to coat the back of a spoon. Discard bay leaf. Stir in thawed peas and sugar snap pea shells; simmer over medium-low heat for 2 minutes.

In a blender (not a food processor), blend sauce until fairly smooth. Strain through a fine sieve into rinsed-out saucepan, discarding solids in sieve. Add sugar snap peas; reheat over medium heat. Remove from heat; stir in remaining butter until melted. Season with salt and pepper to taste; keep warm but do not boil.

Grilled Chicken Breasts: Preheat the oven to 400°F (200°C). Sprinkle chicken breasts on both sides with salt and pepper. In an oiled, ridged ovenproof grill pan over high heat, sear chicken skin side down for 2 to 3 minutes until marked with grill marks. Turn chicken through 90 degrees; sear for 2 to 3 minutes until golden and again nicely marked with grill marks. Turn chicken over. Transfer grill pan to oven; cook for 10 minutes until chicken is tender and juices run clear when thickest breast is pierced with a slim knife. Transfer to a warm platter; let rest, loosely covered, for 5 to 10 minutes.

To Finish: While chicken is cooking, heat 1 tbsp (15 mL) butter in a medium, good-quality, non-stick skillet over medium-high heat. Add mushrooms; cook, stirring often, for 5 minutes, until mushrooms are golden and tender. Reduce heat to medium-low. Scrape risotto into skillet. Add stock to skillet, 1/4 cup (50 mL) at a time, stirring constantly and allowing each batch of stock to be absorbed by rice before adding the next one, until rice is just tender but still *al dente* (you may not need all the stock). Stir in remaining butter, the Parmesan, mascarpone and chives until butter and mascarpone melt. Season with salt and pepper to taste; discard bay leaf.

Meanwhile, in a small skillet over medium heat, cook bacon for 5 to 7 minutes, turning occasionally, until crisp. Drain on paper towels; cut each slice in half crosswise.

To serve, spoon risotto into each of 4 shallow dishes; top each portion with a chicken breast. Drizzle sweet pea emulsion around each dish; garnish with bacon, snow peas, pea shoots and edible flowers.
Makes 4 servings

For the most attractive look, buy skin-on boneless chicken breasts that still have the wing bone attached, if your butcher has them; otherwise use completely boneless breasts with skin. Choose a variety of mushrooms for the risotto, such as morels, chanterelles, hedgehogs, oyster, creminis and shiitake caps. The 2-stage method of cooking the risotto makes it easy to prepare for company.

Grilled Seafood Salad (recipe on page 92)

GRILLED SEAFOOD SALAD

with Antiboise Dressing

Antiboise Dressing:

1/2 cup (125 mL) olive oil

1 tomato, peeled, seeded, cored and diced

2 tbsp (25 mL) finely diced celery

2 tbsp (25 mL) peeled and
finely diced celery root

2 tbsp (25 mL) red wine vinegar

1 tbsp (15 mL) finely chopped shallot

1 tbsp (15 mL) finely chopped basil

1 tbsp (15 mL) finely chopped chervil

1 tbsp (15 mL) finely chopped chives

1-1/2 tsp (7 mL) grated lemon rind

1/4 tsp (1 mL) coriander seeds, cracked

1/4 tsp (1 mL) mustard seeds, cracked

Salt and pepper

Seafood Salad:

1-1/2 lb (750 g) assorted seafood, such as
mussels, salmon fillet, red snapper fillet,
calamari, shelled shrimp and/or sea scallops

2 tbsp (25 mL) olive oil

Salt and pepper

2 cups (500 mL) mesclun
or baby salad greens

Steamed green beans

Potato chips

Antiboise Dressing: In a medium bowl, whisk together oil, tomato, celery, celery root, vinegar, shallot, basil, chervil, chives, lemon rind, coriander and mustard seeds, and salt and pepper to taste; set aside.

Seafood Salad: Preheat the barbecue to medium. Scrub mussels under cold running water, snipping off beards with scissors if necessary and discarding any mussels that don't close when tapped sharply on the counter. Brush salmon, red snapper, calamari and shrimp with olive oil; sprinkle with salt and pepper to taste. Grill salmon and red snapper for 8 to 10 minutes, turning once. Remove from grill; remove any skin if you wish. Keep warm.

Increase heat to high; grill calamari and shrimp for 3 to 4 minutes, turning once, and scallops and mussels for 4 to 6 minutes, turning once and discarding any mussels that don't open.

Divide seafood among 4 plates; drizzle with dressing, dividing evenly. Garnish with mesclun, green beans and potato chips.
Makes 4 servings

Increase the amount of seafood in this colourful appetizer salad to 2 lb (1 kg) and serve as a wonderful main course for a lazy summer's evening.

ROASTED LAMB SIRLOIN

with Summer Ratatouille & Corn Pancakes

Roasted Lamb Sirloin:
1/4 cup (50 mL) olive oil

1 tsp (5 mL) finely chopped shallot

1 tsp (5 mL) minced garlic

1 tsp (5 mL) chopped rosemary

1 tsp (5 mL) chopped thyme

4 boneless lamb sirloin steaks (8 oz/250 g each)

Summer Ratatouille:
1/4 cup (50 mL) olive oil

Half red sweet pepper, seeded and diced

Half yellow sweet pepper, seeded and diced

Half green sweet pepper, seeded and diced

Half 6 oz (175 g) green zucchini, diced

Half 6 oz (175 g) yellow zucchini, diced

Half 12 oz (375 g) eggplant, diced

Half red onion, diced

1 clove garlic, minced

1 tsp (5 mL) grated lemon rind

1 plum tomato, cored, seeded and diced

1/4 cup (50 mL) lightly packed basil leaves, shredded

Salt and pepper

Corn Pancakes:
1 ear corn, shucked

2 eggs, separated

2 tbsp (25 mL) cornstarch

2 tbsp (25 mL) butter, melted

1 tbsp (15 mL) chopped chives

Salt and pepper

Vegetable oil

To Finish:
Salt and pepper

1 tbsp (15 mL) olive oil

Basil leaves

Basil Oil (page 115)

Roasted Lamb Sirloin: In a small bowl, whisk together oil, shallot, garlic, rosemary and thyme. Pat lamb steaks dry on paper towels; put in a shallow dish large enough to hold them in a single layer. Rub on both sides with oil mixture; refrigerate, covered, for 24 hours, turning occasionally.

Summer Ratatouille: In a large pot or Dutch oven, heat oil over medium heat. Add red, yellow and green peppers, green and yellow zucchini, eggplant and onion; cook stirring occasionally, for 8 to 10 minutes until vegetables are starting to soften but are not brown. Stir in garlic and lemon rind; cook, stirring, for 1 minute until fragrant. Stir in tomato and basil, and salt and pepper to taste. Remove from heat; set aside.

Corn Pancakes: With a large, sharp knife, cut kernels from ear of corn. In a small saucepan of boiling salted water, cook corn kernels for 2 minutes; drain through a sieve and immediately immerse in a bowl of ice water. Drain well; pat dry on a clean towel.

Set 1 tbsp (15 mL) corn kernels aside for garnish. In a medium bowl and using a fork, stir together remaining corn kernels, the egg yolks, cornstarch, butter, chives, and salt and pepper to taste. In a separate medium bowl, beat egg whites until stiff peaks form. Gradually fold egg whites into corn mixture until well combined and no white streaks remain.

Oil a large, good-quality, non-stick skillet; heat over medium heat. Spoon batter in 4 heaping 1/3 cup (75 mL) portions into skillet; cook for 3 minutes or until undersides are golden. Turn pancakes over; cook for 2 to 3 minutes until golden on both sides. Remove from skillet; keep warm.

To Finish: Preheat the oven to 400°F (200°C). Remove lamb steaks from marinade; pat dry on paper towels. Sprinkle lamb steaks on both sides with salt and pepper. In a large ovenproof skillet, heat olive oil over medium-high heat. Add lamb steaks; sear for 2 minutes, turning once, until golden brown on both sides. Arrange lamb steaks fat sides up; transfer skillet to oven. Cook for 15 minutes for medium-rare. Remove lamb steaks to a cutting board and cover loosely with foil; let rest for 5 minutes.

Slice lamb steaks thinly; fan out slices on each of 4 plates, dividing evenly. Set a metal ring or cookie cutter on 1 plate. Spoon one-quarter of ratatouille into ring, gently pressing on ingredients to hold them together. Gently push ratatouille onto plate; remove ring. Repeat with remaining ratatouille and plates. Top each stack of ratatouille with a corn pancake; garnish with reserved corn kernels and basil leaves. Spoon a little basil oil around lamb.

Makes 4 servings

Boneless lamb sirloin steaks are cut from the rump end of the leg. You may have to order these from your butcher or, if they're not available, substitute thick-cut bone-in lamb leg steaks instead and after searing, roast for just 8 to 10 minutes.

PEPPERED SEARED TUNA NIÇOISE

Tapenade Dressing:
1/2 cup (125 mL) pitted Niçoise olives,
coarsely chopped
1/4 cup (50 mL) olive oil
1 tbsp (15 mL) coarsely chopped shallot
1 clove garlic, coarsely chopped
Salt and pepper

Salad:
2 blue potatoes (4 oz/125 g each)
6 oz (175 g) fine green beans, trimmed
1/4 cup (50 mL) frozen edamame (shelled
soybeans) or fava beans
1 ear corn, shucked
8 quail eggs
1 tbsp (15 mL) freshly ground black pepper
1 piece (12 oz/375 g) boneless
sushi-grade tuna loin
1/4 cup (50 mL) olive oil
1/4 cup (50 mL) pitted Niçoise olives
4 cherry tomatoes, cut in half crosswise
Salt and pepper
Chives
Edible flowers

Tapenade Dressing: In a mini-chopper or small food processor, pulse olives, oil, shallot and garlic until fairly smooth. Scrape into a small bowl; season with salt and pepper to taste.

Salad: In a steamer set over a saucepan of simmering water, steam potatoes for 20 to 30 minutes until just tender. Remove from heat. When cool enough to handle, remove skin. Cut into quarters lengthwise; set aside.

In a small saucepan of boiling salted water, cook green beans for 2 to 3 minutes until tender-crisp; remove with a slotted spoon and immediately immerse in a bowl of ice water. Add edamame to saucepan; cook for 1 minute; remove with a slotted spoon and add to beans. With a large, sharp knife, cut kernels from ear of corn. Add to saucepan; cook for 1 minute. Drain through a sieve; add to beans.

Meanwhile, put quail eggs in a second small saucepan of simmering water. Bring back to a simmer; cook for 3 minutes; drain. Immediately cool under cold running water. Remove shells; cut eggs in half lengthwise.

Spread pepper out on a large plate. Cut tuna loin in half crosswise; pat dry on paper towels. Roll each piece of tuna in pepper until evenly coated. In a medium skillet, heat 1 tbsp (15 mL) oil over medium-high heat. Add tuna loins; sear, turning often, for 3 to 4 minutes just until seared on all sides (tuna should still be rare in the centre). Remove from skillet; set aside to cool.

Just before serving, cut each piece of tuna crosswise into thin slices. Drain vegetables; pat dry on a clean towel. With your finger and thumb, pop edamame out of their shells, discarding shells. In a large bowl and using your hands, gently toss vegetables, potatoes, olives and tomatoes with remaining olive oil and salt and pepper to taste.

Divide vegetable mixture among 4 plates; top each portion with tuna, dividing evenly. Garnish with quail eggs, chives and edible flowers. Serve tapenade dressing on the side.
Makes 4 servings

The classic salad from southern France gets an update with the addition of blue potatoes, edamame and a piquant black-olive dressing.

GAZPACHO SHOOTERS

6 ripe plum tomatoes,
cored and coarsely chopped
1 red onion, coarsely chopped
1 English cucumber, quartered lengthwise,
seeded and coarsely chopped
1 red sweet pepper,
seeded and coarsely chopped
1 yellow sweet pepper,
seeded and coarsely chopped
1 stalk celery, coarsely chopped
1/2 cup (125 mL) loosely packed basil,
coarsely chopped
4 cloves garlic, coarsely chopped
2 cups (500 mL) canned crushed tomatoes
2 cups (500 mL) V8 Vegetable Cocktail
1/4 cup (50 mL) red wine vinegar
1/4 cup (50 mL) sherry vinegar
1/4 cup (50 mL) olive oil
2 tsp (10 mL) Worcestershire sauce
1/2 tsp (2 mL) Tabasco sauce
Salt and pepper
Edible flowers
Chives

In a very large bowl, stir together tomatoes, red onion, cucumber, red and yellow peppers, celery, basil and garlic. In a food processor, pulse vegetable mixture in batches until very finely minced, scraping down sides of food processor once or twice and transferring each batch to a second very large bowl. Stir canned tomatoes, V8, red wine vinegar, sherry vinegar, oil, and Worcestershire and Tabasco sauces into processed vegetables. Chill well.

Just before serving, season gazpacho with salt and pepper to taste, and more Tabasco if necessary. Ladle into 2 oz (50 mL) shooter glasses; garnish with edible flowers and chives.
Makes about 40 shooter-size servings

Pour this colourful chilled soup into shooter glasses for a great summer hors d'oeuvre for a crowd. Or, if you prefer, ladle it into bowls and serve as a soup course for 6 or 8 people.

JULY
AUGUST
SEPTEMBER

Summertime and I'm in a sunny state of mind. The long awaited local

produce has arrived, filling the marketplace, and offering a host of

possibilities for the inventive cook. I take pleasure in creating

personalized, light, natural cuisine. Dishes that make the most of fresh

flavours and the textures of seasonal ingredients. But also, I take

comfort in preparing old favourites that are forever satisfying to eat.

Enjoy the warm days and evenings of summer and the simple act of

sharing a meal with friends.

CANADA DAY

Imagine the excitement around the Club. Billowing grand flags.

Waving little flags. Everyone becomes one. We are Canada; our

strength is in our character. Understanding and embracing our

differences and reveling in our similarities. Neighbourhoods are

vibrant and alive with red and white festivities. I'm always thrilled.

It's the one day in the year when we all join together out-of-doors to

celebrate a single theme — being Canadian. I'm overwhelmed by a

feeling of pride and wonder. There is a spontaneity all around.

Activities and treats for all ages. To commemorate the occasion, I

have chosen simple, tasty dishes. A salad for an early picnic supper,

or a steak for the backyard party. The recipes are easy to prepare as

friends gather for an early dinner in the warmth of the garden. And

there will be time to view the much anticipated grand finale — the

spectacular fireworks. Happy Birthday Canada!

GRILLED FLANK STEAK

with Tomato Relish & Sweet Potato Wedges

Grilled Flank Steak:

1 flank steak (2 lb/1 kg)

1/4 cup (50 mL) olive oil

3 cloves garlic, minced

2 tbsp (25 mL) chopped chives

2 tbsp (25 mL) chopped parsley

1 tbsp (15 mL) chopped thyme

1/2 tsp (2 mL) black peppercorns, cracked

Salt

Tomato Relish:

7 plum tomatoes, peeled

1 tbsp (15 mL) olive oil

1 cup (250 mL) finely chopped Spanish onion
(one-quarter onion)

2 cloves garlic, minced

1/4 cup (50 mL) packed brown sugar

1/4 cup (50 mL) tomato ketchup

1/4 cup (50 mL) barbeque sauce

2 tbsp (25 mL) grainy Dijon mustard

2 tbsp (25 mL) molasses

2 tbsp (25 mL) finely chopped basil

2 tsp (10 mL) grated lemon rind

Salt and pepper

Sweet Potato Wedges:

4 medium sweet potatoes (3 lb/1.5 kg)

1/4 cup (50 mL) olive oil

Salt and pepper

Grilled Flank Steak: With a small, sharp knife, score steak 2 or 3 times diagonally on both sides. In a small bowl, whisk together oil, garlic, chives, parsley, thyme and peppercorns. Pat flank steak dry on paper towels. Put in a large, shallow dish; rub generously on both sides with oil mixture, rubbing mixture into slashes in steak. Refrigerate, covered, for 24 hours.

Tomato Relish: Core and coarsely chop 5 tomatoes; core, seed and finely dice remainder. In a large, non-reactive saucepan, heat oil over medium heat. Add onion and garlic; cook, stirring often, for 3 to 5 minutes until onion is soft but not brown. Add coarsely chopped tomatoes; cook, covered and stirring occasionally, for 8 to 10 minutes until tomatoes are starting to soften. Stir in brown sugar, ketchup, barbeque sauce, mustard and molasses; simmer, uncovered and stirring often, for 10 to 15 minutes until tomatoes are broken up and mixture has thickened.

Remove from heat; let cool completely. Stir in diced tomatoes, basil, lemon rind, and salt and pepper to taste. Spoon into a medium bowl; refrigerate, covered, until ready to serve.

Sweet Potato Wedges: Preheat the oven to 450°F (230°C). Scrub potatoes but do not peel; cut in half lengthwise. Cut each half lengthwise into 4 wedges. On a large, rimmed baking sheet, toss potato wedges with oil, and salt and pepper to taste. Roast for 15 to 20 minutes, turning once or twice, until browned and tender.

Meanwhile, remove flank steak from refrigerator; preheat the barbecue to medium. Remove flank steak from dish; pat dry on paper towels. Sprinkle on both sides with salt to taste. Grill steak for 8 to 10 minutes, turning once, for medium-rare. Remove to a cutting board; cover loosely with foil and let rest for 5 to 10 minutes. Slice steak thinly across the grain; serve with potato wedges and tomato relish.

Makes 6 servings

The tomato relish that accompanies this flavourful flank steak is also fabulous with grilled chicken or ribs, and any leftovers can be stored in the refrigerator for up to 1 week.

COBB SALAD

with Parmesan Crisps

Parmesan Crisps:
1/2 cup (125 mL) finely grated
Parmesan cheese

Dressing:
1/3 cup (75 mL) olive oil
2 tbsp (25 mL) red wine vinegar
2 tsp (10 mL) finely chopped shallot
2 tsp (10 mL) Dijon mustard
Salt and pepper

Salad:
2 skinless, boneless chicken breasts
(6 oz/175 g each)
Salt and pepper
8 quail eggs
8 cherry tomatoes with stems
1 avocado
1 tbsp (15 mL) lemon juice
2 cups (500 mL) lightly packed, washed,
dried and torn escarole
2 cups (500 mL) lightly packed, washed,
dried and torn frisée
1 Belgian endive, trimmed, cored
and separated into leaves
2 oz (50 g) Fourme d'Ambert cheese,
crumbled and rind removed
Chervil
Chives

Parmesan Crisps: Preheat the oven to 350°F (180°C). Spoon 2 tbsp (25 mL) Parmesan onto a large parchment-paper-lined baking sheet. With your fingers, form into an elongated triangle approximately 5 inches (12 cm) long. Repeat with remaining cheese to make 4 triangles, spacing them 2 inches (5 cm) apart. Bake for 5 minutes or until melted and golden. Let cool completely on baking sheet.

Dressing: In a small bowl, whisk together oil, vinegar, shallot, mustard, and salt and pepper to taste; set aside.

Salad: Preheat the barbecue to medium or heat an oiled, ridged grill pan over medium heat. Sprinkle chicken on both sides with salt and pepper to taste. Grill for 10 to 12 minutes, turning once, until juices run clear when thickest part of chicken is pierced with a slim knife. Remove to a cutting board; let cool completely. Cut chicken thinly into crosswise slices.

Put quail eggs in a small saucepan of simmering water. Bring back to a simmer. Cook for 3 minutes; drain. Immediately cool under cold running water. Remove shells; cut eggs in half crosswise.

Cut a small X in the bottom of each tomato. In a small saucepan of boiling water, blanch tomatoes for 10 seconds. Remove with a slotted spoon and immediately immerse in a bowl of ice water. Remove from water; carefully peel skin from tomatoes without removing it completely so skin resembles petals of a flower, using a small, sharp knife to lengthen splits in skin if necessary; set aside.

Just before serving, cut avocado in half; remove pit. With a 1/2 inch (1 cm) melon baller, scoop balls from 1 avocado half. Remove peel from other half; cut into 1/2 inch (1 cm) cubes. In a small bowl, toss avocado in lemon juice to coat completely.

In the centre of 4 plates, arrange escarole, frisée and endive, dividing evenly. Top greens with chicken breast, drained avocado and cheese, dividing evenly. Arrange quail eggs and cherry tomatoes on top of salads. Whisk dressing; drizzle evenly over each salad. Garnish with parmesan crisps, chervil and chives.
Makes 4 servings

Fourme d'Ambert is a cows milk blue cheese from the Auvergne in central France; it's smooth and creamy with a buttery, not too sharp-tasting flavour.

BISTRO

Quintessential bistro dishes have a familiar face. They are welcoming,

warm and comforting, evoking a sense of timelessness. These recipes

for French comfort food are nourishing and satisfying. They have stood

the test of time to become classics. Bistro cooking is intended for

everyday eating, but it is very important to enjoy the process of

cooking. Don't rush. Use high-quality ingredients and take pleasure in

the preparation. French onion soup, typical bistro fare — you won't

believe how good it is. I always have a feeling of pride and

accomplishment when I serve this dish. The soup is gratifying and

embodies all the components of a great meal — rich cheese, bread,

a sweet vegetable and broth. Simple food and always welcome.

Lobster Bisque (recipe on page 114)   109

LOBSTER BISQUE

6 cooked lobster heads,
tough claws discarded
1 tbsp (15 mL) butter
1 tbsp (15 mL) olive oil
4 tomatoes, cored and diced
2 stalks celery, diced
1 carrot, diced
One-quarter bulb fennel, trimmed, cored and diced
6 cloves garlic, halved
1/3 cup (75 mL) diced shallots
1/4 cup (50 mL) chopped basil
1/4 cup (50 mL) chopped parsley
2 tbsp (25 mL) finely chopped fresh ginger
2 tbsp (25 mL) chopped tarragon
1 tbsp (15 mL) chopped thyme
1 tbsp (15 mL) grated orange rind
2 tsp (10 mL) salt
1 tsp (5 mL) pepper
1/4 tsp (1 mL) crumbled saffron threads
1 cup (250 mL) flour
1/4 cup (50 mL) Cognac
2 tbsp (25 mL) tomato paste
7 cups (1.7 L) Fish Stock (page 216)
1/2 cup (125 mL) white wine
Cognac (optional)
Crème Fraîche (page 217) or sour cream
Chopped tarragon

In a large, deep pot, sturdy metal bowl or a clean pail, pound lobster heads with the end of a wooden rolling pin until finely crushed; set aside.

In a large pot or Dutch oven, heat butter and oil over medium heat. Add tomatoes, celery, carrot, fennel, garlic and shallots; cook, stirring often, for 8 to 10 minutes until vegetables start to soften. Stir in basil, parsley, ginger, tarragon, thyme, orange rind, salt, pepper and saffron; cook, stirring often, for 2 to 3 minutes until fragrant. Stir in lobster shells, flour, Cognac and tomato paste; cook, stirring, for 2 minutes.

Stir in stock and wine; bring to a boil over high heat, stirring often. Reduce heat to medium-low; simmer, covered, for 30 minutes, stirring occasionally, until vegetables are tender. Remove from heat; let cool slightly.

In a blender (not a food processor), blend soup in batches until fairly smooth. Strain through a fine sieve back into rinsed-out pot, putting solids in a medium bowl lined with a double layer of cheesecloth. Gather cheesecloth around solids; squeeze well over pot to extract remaining liquid, discarding solids. Reheat soup gently. Season with more salt and pepper to taste if necessary.

Ladle soup into soup bowls; add a dash of Cognac if you wish. Top each portion with a dollop of crème fraîche; garnish with tarragon.
Makes 6 servings

Save the cooked heads from lobsters you've used in other recipes and store them in the freezer until you have 6, then you can make this fabulous, rich-flavoured soup. For a truly lavish presentation, put cooked lobster meat in each bowl before ladling in the hot soup.

DUNGENESS CRAB CAKES

with Celeriac Remoulade & Red Pepper Coulis

Red Pepper Coulis:

2 red sweet peppers

1 tsp (5 mL) olive oil

Salt and pepper

Celeriac Remoulade:

One-quarter small celery root, peeled and
cut into matchstick strips

1/4 cup (50 mL) mayonnaise

1 tbsp (15 mL) chopped parsley

2 tsp (10 mL) lemon juice

1/2 tsp (2 mL) mustard seeds

Salt and pepper

Basil Oil:

1/2 cup (125 mL) well-packed basil leaves
(stems removed before measuring)

1/2 cup (125 mL) olive oil

Half clove garlic, sliced

Salt and pepper

Crab Cakes:

16 cups (4 L) Court Bouillon (page 216)

1 live Dungeness crab (about 2 lb/1 kg)

1/4 cup (50 mL) cold mashed potato
(one 6 oz/175 g potato)

1 egg yolk

1 tbsp (15 mL) chopped chives

2 tsp (10 mL) chopped parsley

1 tsp (5 mL) grated lemon rind

Salt and pepper

1/3 cup (75 mL) flour

1 egg

3/4 cup (175 mL) panko bread crumbs

2 tbsp (25 mL) butter

1 tbsp (15 mL) olive oil

Salad greens

Red Pepper Coulis: Preheat the broiler to high. Cut peppers in half; arrange cut sides down on a parchment-paper-lined baking sheet. Broil 4 inches (10 cm) from broiler until skins are blackened and blistered all over. Transfer peppers to a bowl; cover tightly with plastic wrap and let stand for at least 10 minutes. When cool enough to handle, remove skin, seeds and white membrane from peppers; chop peppers coarsely.

In a food processor, pulse peppers and olive oil until smooth; rub through a fine sieve, discarding solids in sieve. In a small bowl, stir together peppers and salt and pepper to taste; set aside.

Celeriac Remoulade: In a medium bowl, toss together celery root, mayonnaise, parsley, lemon juice and mustard seeds; season with salt and pepper to taste. Refrigerate, covered, until ready to serve.

Basil Oil: In a small saucepan of boiling water, blanch basil leaves for 30 seconds. With a slotted spoon, remove basil to a bowl of cold water. Drain well; wrap in paper towels and squeeze out excess moisture. Shred basil coarsely. In a blender (not a food processor), combine basil, oil, garlic and salt and pepper to taste; blend until finely minced. Strain through a fine sieve into a small bowl.

Crab Cakes: In a large pot, bring court bouillon to a boil; add crab. Return to a boil. Reduce heat to medium; boil, covered, for 10 minutes. Remove crab; set aside until cool enough to handle. Discard court bouillon.

Set a medium bowl in a larger bowl of ice; use this to hold the crabmeat as you extract it. Holding crab upside down on counter, twist and break claws and legs from body. With kitchen scissors, snip shells open along length of legs; pick out meat with a crab pick or skewer. Crack claws and knuckles with the back of a sturdy knife, taking care not to crush the meat; remove meat.

To open body, lift body away from top shell; discard top shell. With your fingers, carefully remove and discard all of the soft, grey gills (dead men's fingers) from either side of body. With a large, sharp knife, cut body into quarters. Remove the meat from all cavities of the body, discarding any small pieces of membrane. Pick through all the meat in the bowl to ensure there are no pieces of shell. Shred crabmeat into small pieces.

Preheat the oven to 400°F (200°C). Add potato, egg yolk, chives, parsley and lemon rind to crabmeat; stir well. Season with salt and pepper to taste. Form mixture into eight 2 inch (5 cm) patties. Put flour on a plate. Beat egg in a shallow dish; put panko crumbs in a second shallow dish. Coat crab cakes in flour, then in beaten egg; roll in crumbs to coat completely.

Have ready a large baking sheet. In a large, good-quality, non-stick skillet, heat butter and oil over medium-high heat; add crab cakes in a single layer. Sear for 3 minutes, turning once, until golden on both sides. Remove crab cakes to baking sheet; bake for 5 minutes or until crab cakes are hot throughout (check by piercing a cake with a slim knife). Arrange 2 crab cakes on each of 4 plates; spoon celeriac remoulade alongside. Garnish plates with red pepper coulis, basil oil and salad greens.
Makes 4 servings

If you don't have the time or the patience to cook and dismember a crab for these divine crab cakes, substitute 8 oz (250 g) cooked crabmeat, either frozen and thawed or canned.

TRADITIONAL FRENCH ONION SOUP

Soup:
1/4 cup (50 mL) butter
1 tbsp (15 mL) olive oil
3 lb (1.5 kg) onions, thinly sliced
1 cup (250 mL) red wine
1 cup (250 mL) port
1/4 cup (50 mL) balsamic vinegar
8 cups (2 L) Chicken Stock (page 217)
Salt and pepper

Croutons:
1 piece narrow baguette, cut diagonally
into six or eight 1/2 inch (1 cm) slices
2 tbsp (25 mL) olive oil
1 clove garlic, halved
2-1/2 cups (625 mL) shredded Swiss cheese
(approximately 8 oz/250 g)
Rosemary sprigs

Soup: In a very large skillet, heat butter and olive oil over high heat. Add onions; cook for 8 to 10 minutes, stirring occasionally, until edges of onions start to brown. Tip contents of skillet into a large pot or Dutch oven. Cook, uncovered, over medium heat for 30 minutes, stirring occasionally, until onions are very tender and starting to caramelize and bottom of pot is starting to turn dark brown.

Stir in wine, port and vinegar; bring to a boil over high heat, stirring to scrape up any brown bits from bottom of pot. Reduce heat to medium-low; simmer for 5 minutes.

Stir in stock; bring to a boil over high heat. Reduce heat to low; simmer, covered, for 1 hour. Season with salt and pepper to taste.

Croutons: Preheat the oven to 350°F (180°C). Brush bread slices on both sides with olive oil; arrange in a single layer on a baking sheet. Bake for 10 to 12 minutes, turning once, until golden and crisp. Remove from the oven; let cool slightly. Rub 1 side of each slice with cut sides of garlic.

Just before serving, preheat the broiler to high. Set 6 or 8 ovenproof soup bowls on a baking sheet. Ladle soup into bowls; top each serving with 1 crouton. Sprinkle with cheese, dividing evenly. Broil for 2 to 3 minutes until cheese is golden brown and bubbly. Garnish with rosemary sprigs.
Makes 6 to 8 servings

Serve this classic bistro dish before a light main course, or enjoy it alone for lunch or supper.

BARIGOULE OF ARTICHOKES

with Spring Greens

Barigoule of Artichokes:

1 lemon, cut into 8 wedges

4 artichokes (6 oz/175 g each)

1/3 cup (75 mL) olive oil

1 small carrot, finely diced

1 small leek (white and light green parts only), finely diced

2 cloves garlic, halved

3 sprigs thyme

1 bay leaf

1/2 cup (125 mL) white wine

Salt and pepper

1 cup (250 mL) Chicken Stock, plus a little extra if necessary (page 217)

1/2 tsp (2 mL) Dijon mustard

Spring Greens:

1/4 cup (50 mL) olive oil

1 tbsp (15 mL) Champagne vinegar

Salt and pepper

6 cups (1.5 L) lightly packed, washed and dried baby salad greens

Mâche (lamb's lettuce)

Barigoule of Artichokes: Put 4 lemon wedges in a large bowl of cold water. Working with 1 artichoke at a time and being careful of the prickles, snap off all the leaves until a soft cone of inner leaves is revealed. Slice off cone with a sharp knife. Trim end of stem; cut artichoke in half lengthwise and peel stem. Using a teaspoon, scrape out the pointy thistles from the centre. Immediately rub artichoke all over with one of the remaining lemon wedges, coating it well with juice to prevent browning. Drop artichoke and lemon wedge into bowl. Repeat with remaining artichokes and lemon wedges.

In a deep, medium, non-reactive saucepan, heat 1/4 cup (50 mL) oil over medium heat. Add carrot, leek, garlic, thyme and bay leaf; cook, stirring often, for 5 minutes or until vegetables start to soften but are not brown. Drain artichokes and lemon wedges; add both to saucepan, along with wine and salt and pepper to taste, being frugal with the salt as the acidity of the lemon juice and wine will help season the dish. Increase heat to high; boil, uncovered, for 3 to 5 minutes, until wine has evaporated. Discard lemon wedges.

Add stock to saucepan, adding more if necessary so artichokes are just covered. Place a plate over the artichokes to keep them submerged; bring to a boil. Reduce heat to medium-low. Simmer, uncovered, for 10 to 15 minutes, until artichokes are tender when pierced with a knife. Remove from heat; let cool in saucepan.

Drain contents of saucepan through a fine sieve, reserving cooking liquid. Set artichokes, garlic and most of the vegetables aside, discarding remaining vegetables, thyme and bay leaf. In a small bowl, whisk 2 tbsp (25 mL) reserved cooking liquid, remaining oil and mustard until creamy. Season with salt and pepper to taste.

Spring Greens: In a medium bowl, whisk together olive oil, vinegar, and salt and pepper to taste. Add salad greens; toss well. Divide salad among 4 plates. Spoon artichokes and vegetables over salad, dividing evenly. Drizzle reserved cooking liquid over artichokes; garnish with mâche.
Makes 4 servings

This classic way of preparing artichokes makes a lovely spring appetizer. If you prefer, omit the greens and team the versatile artichokes with grilled peppers, olives and other preserved vegetables as part of an antipasti platter, or serve them as an accompaniment to grilled fish.

PAN-SEARED CALF'S LIVER

with Pickled Shallots & Italian Forked Potatoes

Pickled Shallots:

1 cup (250 mL) red wine

1 cup (250 mL) red wine vinegar

1 sprig thyme

1 bay leaf

Pepper and salt

8 small shallots, sliced thinly into rings

Italian Forked Potatoes:

12 medium fingerling potatoes (1-1/2 lb/750 g)

1/4 cup (50 mL) chopped parsley

2 tbsp (25 mL) olive oil

Salt and pepper

Pan-Seared Liver:

1/2 cup (125 mL) flour

1-1/2 lb (750 g) thinly sliced calf's liver

Salt and pepper

1/4 cup (50 mL) butter

2 tbsp (25 mL) olive oil

1 tbsp (15 mL) finely chopped shallot

2 tbsp (25 mL) port

1/2 cup (125 mL) Veal Stock (page 216)

Chervil

Pickled Shallots: In a medium, non-reactive saucepan, stir together wine, vinegar, thyme, bay leaf, 1/2 tsp (2 mL) pepper and 1/4 tsp (1 mL) salt; bring to a boil over high heat. Add shallots; bring back to a boil. Remove saucepan from heat. Pour liquid and shallots into a medium, non-reactive bowl; refrigerate, covered, for up to 24 hours.

Italian Forked Potatoes: In a large saucepan of boiling salted water, cook potatoes for 20 minutes or until just tender. Drain well. Return potatoes to saucepan; shake saucepan over low heat for a few seconds to dry potatoes. Set aside until just cool enough to handle. Peel potatoes; return to saucepan. Mash potatoes roughly with a fork until chunky. Stir in parsley, olive oil, and salt and pepper to taste; keep warm.

Pan-Seared Liver: Strain shallots, reserving 1/3 cup (75 mL) liquid and discarding remaining liquid; set shallots aside. Put flour on a large plate. Sprinkle liver on both sides with salt and pepper; coat on both sides with flour. In a large skillet over medium-high heat, heat 2 tbsp (25 mL) butter and 1 tbsp (15 mL) oil. Sear liver in batches for 2 to 4 minutes (depending on thickness), turning once, until golden on the outside but still pink in the middle, adding up to 1 tbsp (15 mL) butter and the remaining oil to skillet as necessary. Remove liver from skillet as each batch cooks; keep warm.

Drain all fat from skillet. Add reserved shallot pickling liquid and finely chopped shallot to skillet; cook over medium heat for 1 minute, stirring to scrape up any browned bits from bottom of skillet. Standing back in case it ignites, add port to skillet. Stir in stock; bring to a boil. Remove skillet from heat; whisk in remaining 1 tbsp (15 mL) butter until melted. Season with salt and pepper to taste.

Spoon Italian forked potatoes on each of 4 plates; top each portion with liver, dividing evenly. Top liver with pickled shallots; spoon sauce around edge of plate. Garnish with chervil.
Makes 4 servings

Wilted Spinach (page 203) is the perfect accompaniment to succulent calf's liver.

MUSSEL-SAFFRON SOUP

2 lb (1 kg) mussels
4 cloves garlic
5 tbsp (65 mL) olive oil
1-1/2 cups (375 mL) white wine
3 tbsp (45 mL) sliced shallots
1-1/2 tsp (7 mL) chopped thyme
1 tsp (5 mL) chopped rosemary
1/2 cup (125 mL) peeled, finely diced celery root
(one-quarter small root)
1/2 cup (125 mL) finely diced celery (1 stalk)
1/2 cup (125 mL) finely diced fennel
(one-quarter small bulb)
1/2 cup (125 mL) finely diced carrot (1 medium)
1/2 cup (125 mL) finely diced leek (white and light
green parts only of 1 medium)
1/2 cup (125 mL) peeled, finely diced rutabaga
(one-eighth medium rutabaga)
1/4 tsp (1 mL) crumbled saffron threads
3 cups (750 mL) Fish Stock (page 216)
1 tomato, peeled, cored, seeded and finely diced
1 tbsp (15 mL) chopped chives
Salt and pepper
Potato chips
Chives

Scrub mussels under cold running water, snipping off beards with scissors if necessary and discarding any mussels that don't close when tapped sharply on the counter. Finely mince 2 cloves garlic, peeling remainder but leaving them whole.

In a large pot or Dutch oven, heat 2 tbsp (25 mL) oil over medium-high heat. Add mussels, wine, shallots, whole garlic cloves, 1 tsp (5 mL) thyme and 1/2 tsp (2 mL) rosemary; bring to a boil. Cover tightly; cook for 5 minutes or until mussels have opened. Strain through a colander, reserving cooking liquid and mussels separately.

In same pot, heat remaining oil over medium-high heat. Add celery root, celery, fennel, carrot, leek and rutabaga; cook, stirring often, for about 5 minutes until vegetables start to soften but are not brown. Stir in minced garlic, remaining thyme and rosemary, and the saffron; cook, stirring, for 30 seconds until fragrant. Strain reserved mussel cooking liquid through a fine sieve into saucepan; add fish stock. Bring to a boil over high heat. Reduce heat to medium-low; simmer, covered, for 15 minutes until vegetables are just tender.

Meanwhile, remove mussels from their shells, reserving 4 shells for garnish and discarding remaining shells, aromatics and any mussels that haven't opened. Add mussels to saucepan, along with tomato and chives; heat through over low heat. Season with salt and pepper to taste. Ladle soup into 4 warm soup bowls. Set a mussel shell filled with potato chips in each bowl; garnish with chives.
Makes 4 servings

Make your own potato chips (page 58) to garnish this aromatic soup, or cheat and buy good-quality chips.

STEAK TARTARE

with Black Olive Tapenade & Paprika Oil

Paprika Oil:

2 tbsp (25 mL) paprika

1 tbsp (15 mL) finely chopped shallot

1/4 cup (50 mL) canola oil

Black Olive Tapenade:

1/4 cup (50 mL) pitted black olives, coarsely chopped

1 medium plum tomato, peeled, cored, seeded and coarsely chopped

2 tbsp (25 mL) canned tomato sauce

2 anchovy fillets, rinsed, patted dry and coarsely chopped

Steak Tartare:

12 oz (375 g) beef tenderloin

2 tbsp (25 mL) finely chopped shallots

2 tbsp (25 mL) drained capers, rinsed and finely chopped

2 tbsp (25 mL) finely chopped chives

1/2 tsp (2 mL) seeded and minced red chili pepper (or to taste)

1/2 tsp (2 mL) Worcestershire sauce

1/4 tsp (1 mL) Tabasco sauce

Salt and pepper

6 quail eggs

Mustard greens

Sliced baguette

Paprika Oil: In a small, dry skillet over medium heat, cook paprika and shallot for 2 to 3 minutes until fragrant. Stir in oil; heat for 1 to 2 minutes until bubbly. Remove from heat; let stand for 1 hour for flavours to infuse. Strain through a paper-towel-lined sieve into a small bowl; set aside.

Black Olive Tapenade: In a mini-chopper or a small food processor, pulse olives, tomato, tomato sauce and anchovy fillets until fairly smooth, scraping down sides of food processor once or twice. Scrape into a small bowl; set aside.

Steak Tartare: Trim tenderloin of all visible fat. With a large, sharp knife, finely mince tenderloin. Alternatively, coarsely chop tenderloin; then, in a food processor, pulse tenderloin using 6 to 8 one-second pulses until finely minced.

In a medium bowl, stir together tenderloin, shallots, capers, chives, chili pepper, Worcestershire sauce, Tabasco and salt and pepper to taste until well combined. Taste and add more chili pepper, Worcestershire or Tabasco sauces, salt or pepper if necessary.

Set a 2 inch (5 cm) diameter metal ring or cookie cutter on 1 of 6 plates; spoon one-sixth of steak tartare into ring, gently pressing on steak tartare to hold it together. Gently push steak tartare onto plate; remove ring. Repeat with remaining steak tartare and plates. With a teaspoon, make a small indentation in centre of each portion of steak tartare.

Crack 1 quail egg; carefully separate white from yolk, discarding white and retaining yolk in one-half of shell. Set quail shell with yolk in it in indentation on 1 portion of steak tartare. Repeat with remaining quail eggs. Spoon tapenade onto plates, dividing evenly. Garnish with paprika oil and mustard greens. Serve with baguette.
Makes 6 servings

Be sure to buy good-quality beef tenderloin from a reputable butcher for this classic dish.

GRANITE CHICKEN CURRY

Chicken Curry:

3 tbsp (45 mL) vegetable oil

1 cup (250 mL) chopped Spanish onion
(one-quarter onion)

1 stalk celery, chopped

2 tbsp (25 mL) finely chopped fresh ginger

2 tbsp (25 mL) finely chopped lemongrass (1 stalk)

3 cloves garlic, finely chopped

1 can (398 mL) unsweetened coconut milk
(shake well before opening)

1 cup (250 mL) canned diced tomatoes, drained

1/3 cup (75 mL) Indian curry sauce

1-1/2 lb (750 g) boneless, skinless chicken
thighs, trimmed of excess fat and
cut into 1 inch (2.5 cm) pieces

Salt and pepper

Cucumber Raita:

2 plum tomatoes, peeled, cored,
seeded and quartered lengthwise

One-quarter English cucumber, halved lengthwise,
peeled and seeded

One-quarter small red onion

3 tbsp (45 mL) olive oil

1 tbsp (15 mL) lime juice

1/4 cup (50 mL) chopped coriander leaves

Salt and pepper

Basmati Rice:

1-1/2 cups (375 mL) basmati rice

2 cups (500 mL) water

1-1/2 tbsp (22 mL) butter

1 bay leaf

Salt

Poppadoms

Chervil

Chicken Curry: In a medium saucepan, heat 1 tbsp (15 mL) oil over medium heat. Add onion, celery, ginger, lemongrass and garlic; cook, stirring often, for 8 to 10 minutes until onion is soft but not brown. Stir in coconut milk, canned tomatoes and curry sauce; bring to a boil over medium-high heat. Reduce heat to medium-low; cook, uncovered and stirring occasionally, for 20 to 30 minutes until celery is tender. Remove saucepan from heat; let cool slightly. In a blender (not a food processor), blend sauce in batches if necessary until fairly smooth. Rub through a fine sieve into rinsed-out saucepan, discarding solids in sieve; set sauce aside.

In a large skillet, heat 1 tbsp (15 mL) oil over medium-high heat. Sprinkle chicken with salt and pepper; sear chicken in batches and add more oil to skillet as necessary for 3 to 4 minutes, turning often, until golden (chicken will not be completely cooked). Remove each batch from skillet with a slotted spoon and add to sauce.

Bring sauce to a boil over medium-high heat. Reduce heat to medium-low; simmer uncovered and stir occasionally for 10 to 12 minutes until largest pieces of chicken are no longer pink inside. Season with salt and pepper to taste; keep warm.

Cucumber Raita: Cut tomatoes, cucumber and onion crosswise into thin slices. In a large bowl, whisk together oil and lime juice. Stir in tomatoes, cucumber, onion and coriander. Season with salt and pepper to taste; set aside.

Basmati Rice: In a medium bowl, rinse rice in cold water, swirling rice with your fingers and changing water frequently until it's almost clear; drain well. In a medium saucepan with a tight-fitting lid, stir together rice, water, 1/2 tbsp (7 mL) butter, the bay leaf and 1/2 tsp (2 mL) salt. Bring to a boil over high heat. Reduce heat to medium-low; simmer, covered, for 15 minutes. Remove from heat; let stand, without lifting lid, for 10 minutes. Add remaining butter; fluff with a fork.

Spoon rice into 4 shallow bowls; top with curry, dividing evenly. Spoon cucumber raita over curry; garnish with poppadoms and chervil.
Makes 4 servings

Here's a great classic that's been a fixture at the Granite Club practically forever and woe betide the chef who tries to take it off the menu! Look for curry sauce – not paste – for this recipe. Most large supermarkets sell good-quality curry sauce; the one I use is, strangely, a Chinese brand from a company called Chiseng.

PARMA HAM & MELON

with Tarragon-Yogurt Dressing

1/2 cup (125 mL) plain yogurt
1 tbsp (15 mL) finely chopped shallot
1 tbsp (15 mL) chopped tarragon
1 tbsp (15 mL) tarragon vinegar
Salt and pepper
1 large cantaloupe
One-half large honeydew melon
One-quarter seedless watermelon
18 slices prosciutto (about 9 oz/275 g)
Mâche (lamb's lettuce)

In a glass measure, stir together yogurt, shallot, tarragon, vinegar, and salt and pepper to taste until smooth.

Scrub rinds of all melons; dry thoroughly. Cut cantaloupe into 6 wedges, removing seeds; cut rind from each wedge. Cut a 4 x 2 inch (10 x 5 cm) triangle from each wedge, reserving trimmings. Repeat with honeydew melon.

Cut watermelon into four 1/2 inch (1 cm) slices; cut rind from slices. Cut two 4 x 2 inch (10 x 5 cm) triangles from each of 3 slices, reserving 4th slice.

With a melon baller (use ballers of different sizes if you have them), scoop 12 balls each from cantaloupe and honeydew trimmings and reserved slice of watermelon to make a total of 36 balls.

To serve, stand 3 triangles of melon, using 1 of each kind for each portion, vertically on each of 6 individual plates, trimming bases so they stand up. Arrange prosciutto on each platter, threading slices around melon triangles. Garnish each portion with melon balls, mâche and a spoonful of tarragon-yogurt dressing.
Makes 6 servings

This is a great classic for the summer and I've had fun being creative with this dish by using 3 varieties of melon.

CITRUS SAMPLER TRIO

Agrume Terrine:

4 oranges

1-1/2 tsp (7 mL) grated lemon rind

4 blood oranges

4 red grapefruit

1 cup (250 mL) sugar

2/3 cup (150 mL) water

1 envelope (7 g) unflavoured
powdered gelatine

Frozen Lemon Soufflés:

1 large lemon

2 eggs

4 egg yolks

1/3 cup (75 mL) sugar

1 envelope (7 g) unflavoured
powdered gelatine

1 cup (250 mL) whipping cream

Blood Orange Sorbet:

5 to 6 blood oranges

1 cup (250 mL) water

1 cup (250 mL) sugar

1 tbsp (15 mL) lemon juice

Chopped pistachios

Raspberry Sauce (page 59)

Fresh berries

Citrus rind

Mint sprigs

Agrume Terrine: Grate the rind from 1 orange. In a small bowl, stir together orange and lemon rinds; cover and set aside. With a small, sharp knife, and holding fruit over a bowl to catch the juice, cut rind and white pith from all oranges, blood oranges and grapefruit. Continuing to hold fruit over bowl, cut segments away from membranes, letting them drop into bowl. Squeeze membranes to extract juice. Strain segments through a colander, reserving juice. Put segments in a large, non-reactive bowl. In a small saucepan, stir together sugar and water; bring to a boil over medium-high heat. Pour over segments; refrigerate, covered, overnight.

Strain citrus segments through a colander, reserving sugar syrup. Arrange grapefruit segments in base of a 6 cup (1.5 L) terrine or loaf pan; sprinkle with one-third orange and lemon rind. Top with orange segments, then blood orange segments, sprinkling each layer with one-third of citrus rind. Pour 1/3 cup (75 mL) reserved citrus juice into a glass measure, discarding remaining juice. Sprinkle gelatine over surface of juice; let stand for 5 minutes until puffy. Meanwhile, in a small saucepan, heat 3/4 cup (175 mL) reserved sugar syrup over medium-high heat until simmering; discard remaining syrup. Pour hot sugar syrup over gelatine, whisking until gelatine has completely dissolved. Pour gelatin mixture evenly into loaf pan; refrigerate, covered, overnight.

Frozen Lemon Soufflés: Cut six 1-1/2 inch (4 cm) wide strips of foil, each long enough to wrap around a 1/3 cup (75 mL) espresso cup. Wrap around 6 espresso cups so foil stands 1 inch (2.5 cm) above rims; secure with tape. Grate rind and squeeze juice from lemon. In a large bowl and using an electric mixer, beat eggs, egg yolks and sugar for about 3 minutes until thick and pale; beat in lemon rind and juice. Pour 2 tbsp (25 mL) cold water into a small bowl; sprinkle gelatine over surface. Let stand for 5 minutes until puffy; put bowl in a saucepan containing enough barely simmering water to come halfway up side of bowl. Heat, stirring often, for 1 minute or until gelatine is completely dissolved. Fold gelatine mixture into egg mixture.

In a medium bowl, whip cream until soft peaks form. Gradually fold cream into egg mixture until no white streaks remain. Spoon mixture into prepared espresso cups, dividing evenly. Freeze for 2 to 3 hours until firm. (If frozen for longer, let stand at room temperature for 30 minutes to soften slightly before serving.)

Blood Orange Sorbet: Segment oranges as described above. In a food processor, pulse orange segments and juice until fairly smooth. Measure 2 cups (500 mL) orange purée into a medium bowl, discarding remainder; whisk in water, sugar and lemon juice until sugar has dissolved. Chill well.

Pour orange mixture into an ice cream maker and churn according to manufacturer's instructions. Alternatively, pour into a shallow 6 cup (1.5 L) container (preferably metal); freeze, covered, for 2 to 3 hours until a 1 inch (2.5 cm) frozen border has formed around edge. Scrape sorbet into a food processor; pulse until smooth. Scrape back into container; freeze, covered, for about 5 hours until firm.

To serve, remove foil collars from espresso cups; garnish with pistachios and fresh berries. Set 1 on each of 6 individual dessert platters. Run a knife around inside edge of terrine pan; dip base of pan in hot water for a few seconds. Invert onto cutting board. Cut terrine crosswise into slices. Place a slice of terrine on each dessert platter; garnish with citrus rind. Add a scoop of sorbet. Drizzle with raspberry sauce; garnish with mint.
Makes 6 servings

Here's a stunning presentation of 3 refreshing citrus-spiked desserts that are surprisingly easy to make.

CHEF'S TABLE

A passion for fish and for marrying elements from the garden and the sea are truly my first culinary loves. Inspiration for this collection of dishes comes from my time spent on the coast of Normandy and in Marseille in Provence. Imagine eating bouillabaisse on the docks of Marseille, prepared with seafood caught in the Mediterranean that very morning. Or sitting down to enjoy Mediterranean sea bass — the morning catch — from the Quai des Belges in the old port — a delicately flavoured fish served with black truffles of Perigord. Normandy, the land of Camembert, cream and butter. Everywhere you will be offered Tarte aux Pommes, created with local ingredients and served with cider or the powerful apple brandy known as Calvados. In honour of a true Norman, my friend Laurent Cesne of Hôtel Restaurant de la Marine in Barneville-Carteret, I have chosen to include caramelized apple tart as part of the Chef's Table repertoire. Vive la Normandie!

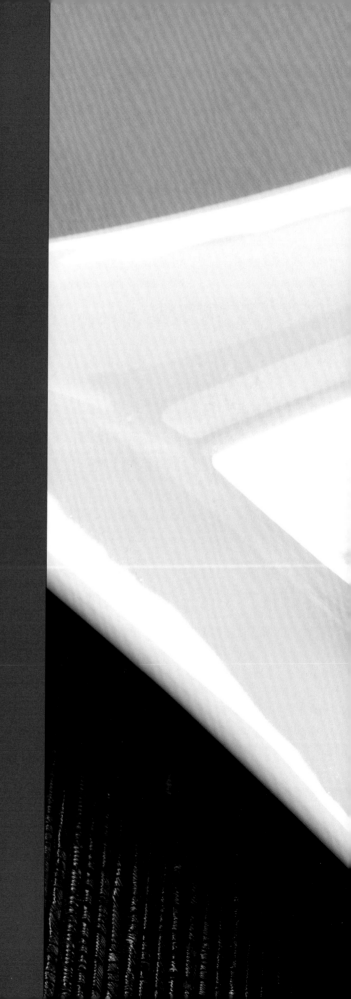

ROASTED TURBOT

with Spring Vegetable Frou-Frou & Nantaise Butter

Spring Vegetable Frou-Frou:
1 lemon, cut into quarters

2 baby artichokes (3 oz/75 g each)

4 baby green zucchini

1/2 cup (125 mL) frozen edamame (shelled
soybeans), thawed

16 fine green beans

4 baby yellow patty pan squash

4 baby carrots

4 broccoflower or broccoli florets

Salt and pepper

1-1/2 cups (375 mL) shredded Savoy cabbage
(one-quarter of a head)

4 cherry tomatoes

Nantaise Butter:
1/2 cup (125 mL) red wine vinegar

2 tbsp (25 mL) finely chopped shallots

1 tbsp (15 mL) whipping cream

1/2 cup (125 mL) butter, cubed

Salt and pepper

Roasted Turbot:
3 tbsp (45 mL) olive oil

2 tbsp (25 mL) white wine

1 tsp (5 mL) grated lemon rind

4 bone-in turbot steaks (8 oz/250 g each)

Salt and pepper

Fennel fronds

Spring Vegetable Frou-Frou: Put 2 lemon wedges in a medium bowl of cold water. Working with 1 artichoke at a time and being careful of the prickles, snap off all outer leaves until a soft cone of inner leaves is revealed. Slice about 1/2 inch (1 cm) from top of cone with a sharp knife. Trim end of stem; cut artichoke in half lengthwise and peel stem. Immediately rub artichoke all over with 1 of the remaining lemon wedges, coating it well with juice to prevent browning. Drop artichoke and lemon wedge into bowl. Repeat with remaining artichoke and lemon wedge.

Cut each zucchini lengthwise almost but not quite through so that slices fan out. With your finger and thumb, pop edamame beans out of their shells, discarding shells. Drain artichokes. In a steamer set over a large saucepan of simmering water, steam artichokes, zucchini, green beans, squash, carrots and broccoflower florets for 5 to 12 minutes, depending on variety, until just tender (check frequently and remove each vegetable as it cooks). Season with salt and pepper to taste; keep warm.

Meanwhile, in a medium saucepan of boiling water, blanch cabbage and edamame beans for 3 to 5 minutes until just tender. With a slotted spoon, remove from saucepan; keep warm. Leave saucepan over heat.

Remove stalks from tomatoes and cut a small X in the bottom of each. Add tomatoes to saucepan of boiling water; blanch for 10 seconds. Remove with a slotted spoon and immediately immerse in a bowl of ice water. Remove from water; carefully peel skin from tomatoes without removing it completely so skin resembles petals of a flower, using a small, sharp knife to lengthen splits in skin if necessary; set aside.

Nantaise Butter: In a small saucepan, combine vinegar and shallots; bring to a boil over medium-high heat. Boil for 4 to 6 minutes until liquid has almost all evaporated. Stir in cream. Remove from heat; gradually whisk in butter one cube at a time until melted, returning saucepan to low heat halfway through adding butter. Season with salt and pepper to taste; keep warm but do not boil.

Roasted Turbot: In a small bowl, whisk together 2 tbsp (25 mL) olive oil, the white wine and lemon rind. Put turbot in a shallow dish large enough to hold it more or less in a single layer. Rub olive oil mixture evenly over both sides of fish; set aside for 10 minutes, turning after 5 minutes.

Preheat the oven to 400°F (200°C). In a large ovenproof skillet, heat remaining oil over medium-high heat. Remove turbot from marinade; sprinkle on both sides with salt and pepper to taste. Add turbot to skillet; sear for 3 minutes, turning once, until golden brown on both sides. Transfer skillet to the oven; bake for 5 minutes until turbot is firm to the touch. If you wish, remove bones and skin from fish before serving; keep warm.

To serve, divide cabbage and edamame beans among 4 plates; top with remaining vegetables (except green beans), dividing evenly. Top each portion of vegetables with turbot, dividing evenly. Arrange green beans on top of fish, dividing evenly. Spoon Nantaise butter around each portion; garnish with fennel fronds.
Makes 4 servings

Turbot is mild-flavoured flatfish popular in Europe. I buy my turbot live from a store in Toronto's Chinatown but bone-in halibut steaks can be substituted if you wish.

SEA BASS ALPILLES

1 English cucumber

1 green zucchini (6 oz/175 g)

1 yellow zucchini (6 oz/175 g)

One-quarter bulb fennel, trimmed and
tough core removed

1 cup (250 mL) olive oil

4 tsp (20 mL) coriander seeds, cracked

1-1/2 tsp (7 mL) black peppercorns, cracked

1-1/2 tsp (7 mL) grated lemon rind

Salt

3 tomatoes, peeled, cored, seeded and diced

1/2 cup (125 mL) butter, clarified (page 18)

4 sea bass fillets (5 oz/150 g each)

1/2 cup (125 mL) Fish Stock (page 216)

2 tbsp (25 mL) white wine

1 small black truffle, sliced (optional)

1/4 cup (50 mL) chopped basil

4 sprigs chervil

Black truffles

Peel cucumber, discarding skin. Using a mandolin slicer fitted with a shredding blade, shred cucumber, discarding its central core of seeds. Put cucumber shreds in a medium bowl. Shred peel from green and yellow zucchini, reserving rest of zucchini for use in another recipe (such as stock). Add zucchini peel to cucumber.

Fit mandolin with slicing blade; finely shave fennel. Add fennel to cucumber. In a large, non-reactive bowl, whisk all but 2 tbsp (25 mL) olive oil with 3 tsp (15 mL) coriander seeds, 1 tsp (5 mL) peppercorns, the lemon rind and salt to taste. Add cucumber mixture and tomatoes; stir well. Cover and set aside at room temperature for up to 2 hours for flavours to blend.

To serve, preheat the oven to 450°F (230°C). Pour half of the butter into a shallow, ovenproof dish large enough to hold the sea bass in a single layer. Sprinkle half of the remaining coriander seeds and peppercorns, and salt to taste over base of dish. Arrange sea bass in dish; sprinkle with remaining coriander seeds and peppercorns, and salt to taste. Pour fish stock, wine and remaining olive oil around fish; drizzle fish with remaining butter. Top fish with truffles, dividing evenly among fillets. Cover dish tightly with foil; bake for 18 to 20 minutes until fish is just firm to the touch.

Remove fish to a warm platter without dislodging truffles, reserving cooking juices in dish. Remove skin from fish if you wish; keep fish warm.

Tip vegetables and their marinade into a large, non-reactive saucepan; add cooking juices from baking dish. Heat over medium heat for 2 to 3 minutes, stirring occasionally, until vegetables are just warm. Remove from heat; gently stir in basil.

Using tongs, divide vegetables among 4 shallow bowls. Spoon some of the liquid from saucepan over vegetables. Top each portion of vegetables with a piece of fish; drizzle fish with some of the remaining juices from saucepan. Garnish with chervil and black truffles.

Makes 4 servings

Marinated vegetables teamed with sea bass fillets perfectly captures the flavours of Provence. This was one of my favourite dishes when I worked alongside Gérald Passédat at Le Petit Nice, a 2-star Michelin hôtel restaurant in Marseille, in the south of France.

SEARED ST. PIERRE

with Spiced Fennel & Lemon Relish

Lemon Relish:

1/3 cup (75 mL) water

3 tbsp (45 mL) sugar

3 lemons

3 cloves

2 bay leaves

1 star anise

Half cinnamon stick

Chervil-Anise Nage:

1 bulb fennel

2 tbsp (25 mL) butter

1/2 cup (125 mL) coarsely chopped shallots

2 cloves garlic, coarsely chopped

6 sprigs thyme tied together with kitchen string

2 bay leaves

2 star anise

1 cup (250 mL) white wine

2 cups (500 mL) Fish Stock (page 216)

1/4 cup (50 mL) whipping cream

1/4 cup (50 mL) chopped chervil

Spiced Fennel:

1 tbsp (15 mL) butter

1/2 cup (125 mL) Chicken Stock (page 216)

2 bay leaves

1 star anise

St. Pierre:

4 boneless, skinless St. Pierre fillets

(5 oz/150 g each; see note below)

Salt and pepper

1 tbsp (15 mL) butter

1 tsp (5 mL) olive oil

Sliced, cooked new potatoes

Fennel Slaw (page 82)

Lemon Relish: In a small saucepan, stir together water and sugar; bring to a boil over medium-high heat. Remove from heat; set aside. With a citrus zester, remove rind from lemons in long, thin strips, avoiding white pith. Cut lemons in half and squeeze juice into saucepan containing sugar syrup, discarding pips but adding any squeezed pulp. In a separate small saucepan of boiling water, blanch lemon rind for 2 minutes; drain well. Add lemon rind to sugar syrup, along with cloves, bay leaves, star anise and cinnamon stick. Bring to a boil over high heat. Reduce heat to medium; boil for 25 minutes, stirring occasionally, until reduced to 1/4 cup (50 mL) and relish is syrupy. Remove from heat; discard spices and bay leaves. Pour relish into a small bowl; let cool completely. Warm slightly before serving so relish is easy to spoon.

Chervil-Anise Nage: Trim tops from fennel but leave root end intact; remove any remaining leaves, reserving tops and leaves. Cut fennel in half lengthwise; cut each half lengthwise into 3 pieces, removing and reserving core. Set aside 2 pieces for fennel slaw (page 82); trim remaining pieces of fennel so they're evenly shaped like footballs, reserving trimmings as before. Set pieces of fennel aside for spiced fennel (recipe follows).

Reserving 4 leafy fronds for garnish, coarsely chop all fennel trimmings, keeping leaves separate. In a wide, medium saucepan, melt 1 tbsp (15 mL) butter over medium heat. Add all fennel trimmings except leaves, the shallots, garlic, thyme, bay leaves and star anise; cook, stirring often, for 3 to 5 minutes until shallots are softened but not brown. Add wine; bring to a boil over high heat. Reduce heat to medium; boil for 8 minutes or until liquid has reduced to 1/2 cup (125 mL). Add fish stock; bring to a boil over high heat. Reduce heat to medium; boil for 1 hour, 15 minutes or until liquid has reduced to 1 tbsp (15 mL) and is syrupy. Add cream; boil for 1 minute until thickened slightly. Remove from heat.

Remove and discard thyme, bay leaves and star anise; stir in chervil and reserved fennel leaves. In a food processor, pulse sauce until smooth. Strain through a fine sieve into a small saucepan. Reheat before serving but do not boil. Remove from heat; whisk in remaining butter. Season with salt and pepper to taste.

Spiced Fennel: In a medium saucepan large enough to hold reserved fennel from chervil-anise nage in a single layer, melt butter over medium heat. Add fennel; sprinkle with salt and pepper to taste. Cook for 5 to 7 minutes, turning often, until golden on all sides. Add chicken stock, bay leaves and star anise; bring to a boil over high heat. Reduce heat to medium; simmer, uncovered, for 20 minutes, turning fennel occasionally, until it is tender and chicken stock is reduced. Season with salt and pepper to taste; keep warm.

St. Pierre: Cut fillets in half; sprinkle on both sides with salt and pepper to taste. In a large, good-quality, non-stick skillet, heat butter and oil over medium-high heat. Cook fillets for 6 to 8 minutes, turning once, until firm. Divide potatoes among 6 plates; top each portion with 2 pieces of St. Pierre fillet. Top fish with glazed fennel. Spoon fennel slaw on top of each piece of glazed fennel; top each with a spoonful of lemon relish. Drizzle plates with chervil-anise nage; garnish with reserved fennel fronds.
Makes 4 servings

St. Pierre is a mild-tasting white fish also known as John Dory. If your fishmonger only has whole fish, you'll need one that weighs about 3-1/2 lb (1.75 kg); ask him to fillet the fish into 4 portions, retaining the bones and other trimmings for stock. Grouper fillets can also be used in this recipe.

ROASTED MONKFISH

with Salade Vierge & Cashew Couscous

Salade Vierge:

1/2 cup (125 mL) olive oil

20 pieces Oven-Dried Plum Tomato (page 217)

3 yellow tomatoes, seeded and diced

1 medium green zucchini, diced (6 oz/175 g)

1/2 cup (125 mL) pitted Niçoise olives

1/4 cup (50 mL) drained, rinsed capers

3 tbsp (45 mL) finely chopped shallots

3 tbsp (45 mL) chopped basil

3 tbsp (45 mL) chopped parsley

3 cloves garlic, minced

1 tsp (5 mL) grated lemon rind

Salt and pepper

Cashew Couscous:

1/4 cup (50 mL) olive oil

3 tbsp (45 mL) finely chopped shallots

2 cloves garlic, minced

1 tsp (5 mL) ground cumin

3/4 tsp (4 mL) ground coriander

1-3/4 cups (425 mL) Chicken Stock (page 217)

1/3 cup (75 mL) sultanas

1-1/2 cups (375 mL) couscous

1/2 cup (125 mL) unsalted roasted cashew nuts, coarsely chopped and toasted

2 tbsp (25 mL) chopped basil

2 tbsp (25 mL) chopped coriander

2 tbsp (25 mL) chopped mint

Salt and pepper

Roasted Monkfish:

2 bone-in monkfish tails (1-1/2 lb/750 g each), skin removed

1/4 cup (50 mL) flour

Salt and pepper

2 tbsp (25 mL) olive oil

1 tbsp (15 mL) butter

1 large whole head garlic, separated into individual cloves

Chervil

Salade Vierge: In a medium, non-reactive bowl, stir together olive oil, dried and yellow tomatoes, zucchini, olives, capers, shallots, basil, parsley, garlic and lemon rind; season with salt and pepper to taste. Refrigerate, covered, until ready to serve.

One hour before serving, remove bowl of salade vierge from refrigerator; let stand at room temperature. Just before serving, set bowl of salad over a saucepan of hot water; let stand for 10 to 15 minutes, stirring occasionally, until salad is lukewarm.

Cashew Couscous: In a medium saucepan, heat 1 tbsp (15 mL) oil over medium-high heat. Add shallots; cook, stirring, for 3 to 5 minutes until shallots are softened but not brown. Add garlic, cumin and coriander; cook, stirring, for 1 minute. Add chicken stock and sultanas; bring to a boil over high heat. Remove from heat. Stir in couscous; let stand, covered, for 5 minutes. Fluff with a fork; stir in cashews, basil, coriander, mint and remaining olive oil. Season with salt and pepper to taste. Keep warm.

Roasted Monkfish: Preheat the oven to 400°F (200°C). With a small, sharp knife, cut off the thin membrane covering each monkfish tail. Cut each tail crosswise into three 2 inch (5 cm) pieces, reserving skinny ends for use in fish stock. Put flour in a shallow dish. Sprinkle monkfish pieces on all sides with salt and pepper; roll in flour to coat completely. In a large, ovenproof skillet, heat oil and butter over medium-high heat. Add monkfish and garlic; sear for 4 minutes, turning monkfish often and stirring garlic, until monkfish is golden on all sides. Transfer skillet to the oven; bake for 12 minutes or until thickest part of monkfish feels very tender when pierced with a slim knife.

To serve, spoon couscous in centre of each of 4 plates; top each portion with a piece of monkfish. Spoon salade vierge around edge of plate; garnish with roasted garlic and chervil.

Makes 6 servings

Monkfish is probably one of the ugliest fish in the sea but you need only the meaty tails for this dish and it's likely your fishmonger will have already dealt with its huge ungainly head! A firm-textured fish with a rich taste similar to lobster, it's only tender when thoroughly cooked.

Bouillabaisse (recipe on page 146)

BOUILLABAISSE

Rouille:

3 egg yolks

4 cloves garlic, coarsely chopped

1 tsp (5 mL) seeded and chopped hot red chili pepper

Half stalk lemongrass, trimmed and coarsely chopped

1/2 tsp (2 mL) crumbled saffron threads

Salt

1/2 cup (125 mL) olive oil

1/4 cup (50 mL) vegetable oil

2 tbsp (25 mL) lemon juice

Bouillabaisse:

1/2 cup (125 mL) olive oil

2 cups (500 mL) diced carrots (2 large)

1 cup (250 mL) diced fennel (one-quarter bulb)

1 cup (250 mL) peeled, diced rutabaga (one-eighth rutabaga)

1 cup (250 mL) diced celery (2 stalks)

1 cup (250 mL) peeled, diced celery root (one-quarter small root)

1 cup (250 mL) seeded, cored and diced tomatoes (2 medium)

9 cloves garlic, halved

1 tbsp (15 mL) chopped rosemary

1 tbsp (15 mL) chopped thyme

6 star anise

1 tsp (5 mL) salt

1 tsp (5 mL) pepper

1 tsp (5 mL) crumbled saffron threads

6 medium potatoes (1-1/4 lb/625 g), peeled and cut into 1/2 inch (1 cm) slices

6 cups (1.5 L) Fish Stock (page 216)

2 cups (500 mL) Lobster Bisque (page 114)

1/2 cup (125 mL) white wine

1/4 cup (50 mL) Ricard or Pernod

2-1/4 lb (1.1 kg) assorted fish and seafood

1/4 cup (50 mL) finely chopped chervil

1/4 cup (50 mL) finely chopped chives

2 tbsp (25 mL) finely chopped parsley

1 baguette

Chervil

Cooked langoustine claws

Rouille: In a blender (not a food processor), blend egg yolks, garlic, chili pepper, lemongrass, saffron and salt to taste until finely minced. With the motor running, gradually add olive and vegetable oils and lemon juice through lid until mixture is smooth, creamy and the consistency of mayonnaise. Scrape into a bowl; refrigerate, covered, until ready to serve.

Bouillabaisse: In a large pot or Dutch oven, heat oil over medium heat. Add carrots, fennel, rutabaga, celery, celery root, tomatoes, 8 cloves garlic, rosemary, thyme, star anise, salt, pepper and saffron; cook, stirring, for 2 to 3 minutes until fragrant. Add potatoes; cook, stirring often, for 8 to 10 minutes until vegetables start to soften. Stir in stock, lobster bisque, wine and Ricard; bring to a boil over high heat. Reduce heat to medium-low; simmer, uncovered, for 10 to 15 minutes until potatoes are tender but not broken up. Remove from heat; let stand at room temperature for 1 hour for flavours to infuse.

Just before serving, bring contents of pot back to a boil over high heat. Reduce heat to medium; boil, uncovered, for 5 minutes. Increase heat to high; stir in fish and seafood. Remove pot from heat; let stand, covered, for 10 to 15 minutes until shrimp are pink and fish and seafood are just firm. Stir in chervil, chives and parsley. Season with more salt and pepper to taste if necessary.

Meanwhile, slice baguette diagonally into 1/2 inch (1 cm) slices. Toast slices on both sides; rub with reserved garlic. Ladle bouillabaisse into deep soup bowls, making sure everyone gets a selection of fish and seafood; garnish bowls with chervil and langoustine claws. Serve with toasted baguette and rouille on the side.
Makes 6 servings

Choose a selection of fish and seafood – sea bass, Dover sole, turbot, salmon, red snapper or pickerel fillets, mussels, calamari, large shrimp and/or scallops are all good – for this classic main-course soup. Allow 6 oz (175 g) per person and cut the fish fillets into pieces the same size as the shrimp.

CARAMELIZED APPLE TARTS

1 pkg (397 g) frozen puff pastry, thawed
2 tbsp (25 mL) sugar
1/2 tsp (2 mL) ground cinnamon
3 Granny Smith apples (1 lb 5 oz/650 g)
1/4 cup (50 mL) butter, melted
1/4 cup (50 mL) apricot jam
Vanilla Ice Cream (page 59)
Mint sprigs

Preheat the oven to 400°F (200°C). Line a very large baking sheet (or 2 large baking sheets) with parchment paper. On a lightly floured surface, roll out half of the pastry to an 11 inch (28 cm) square. Using a saucer or small plate as a guide, cut out four 5 inch (12 cm) circles from pastry. Transfer to baking sheet; prick pastry circles all over with a fork. Repeat with remaining pastry.

In a small bowl, stir together sugar and cinnamon; set aside. Peel, core and quarter apples. Using a mandolin slicer, cut apple quarters into wafer-thin slices. Arrange slices decoratively and overlapping slightly on pastry circles to cover pastry completely. Brush apples with butter; sprinkle with cinnamon sugar. Bake for 20 to 30 minutes until apples are caramelized and edges of tarts are golden, switching position of baking sheets halfway through cooking time if using 2 sheets.

Meanwhile, in a small saucepan, heat jam over medium heat until melted. Brush each tart with jam. Serve hot with vanilla ice cream; garnish with mint sprigs.
Makes 8 servings

Patisserie-style tarts like these are so quick to make they're sure to become part of your repertoire.

NIAGARA FRUIT FESTIVAL

Au naturel — fresh plump fruit, just picked, still warm from the summer sun. When perfectly ripe and in season it is one of the nicest ways to finish a meal. I always include a selection of cheeses to accompany the fruit. It is a perfect marriage of flavours. Perhaps pear with Brie or plum with St. André, or even apple with Camembert à la Normande.

From Niagara's orchards there is nothing like a sweet peach or a juicy pear to inspire a spectacular dessert. One that seduces you and plays with your sense of taste, leaving you wanting more.

ROASTED NIAGARA PEACH SOLEIL

Basil Sorbet:

5 cups (1.2 L) lightly packed basil leaves

1 cup plus 2 tbsp (275 mL) orange juice

1 cup (250 mL) ice cubes

2 tsp (10 mL) unsweetened powdered gelatine

3/4 cup (175 mL) sugar

1/2 cup (125 mL) lemon juice

1/3 cup (75 mL) glucose syrup

Almond Cream:

1/2 cup (125 mL) almond flour

1/4 cup (50 mL) sugar

1/4 cup (50 mL) sifted cake-and-pastry flour

1/4 cup (50 mL) butter, softened

1 egg

2 tsp (10 mL) dark rum (optional)

Pastries:

1 egg

2 pkgs (397 g each) frozen puff pastry, thawed

4 firm ripe peaches,
pitted and each cut into 16 wedges

2 tbsp (25 mL) icing sugar

Pastry Cream (page 217)

Basil leaves

Basil Sorbet: In a blender (not a food processor), blend basil, 1 cup (250 mL) orange juice and ice cubes until finely minced; strain through a fine sieve into a large bowl. In a medium bowl, sprinkle gelatine over surface of remaining orange juice; let stand for 5 minutes until puffy. Meanwhile, in a small saucepan, heat sugar, lemon juice and glucose syrup over medium-high heat until bubbly. Pour hot sugar mixture over gelatine mixture, whisking until gelatine has completely dissolved. Stir sugar mixture into basil mixture; chill well.

Pour basil mixture into an ice cream maker and churn according to manufacturer's instructions. Alternatively, pour into a shallow 6 cup (1.5 L) container (preferably metal); freeze, covered, for 2 to 3 hours until a 1 inch (2.5 cm) frozen border has formed around edge. Scrape sorbet into a food processor; pulse until smooth. Scrape back into container; freeze, covered, for about 5 hours until firm.

Almond Cream: In a small bowl, stir together almond flour, sugar and cake-and-pastry flour. In a medium bowl and using an electric mixer, beat butter until smooth and fluffy. Beat in half of almond flour mixture; beat in egg. Beat in remaining almond flour mixture until smooth and well combined. Beat in rum; set aside.

Pastries: In a small bowl, beat egg with 1 tbsp (15 mL) cold water. On a lightly floured surface, roll out one-quarter of puff pastry (half a package) to an 11 inch (28 cm) square. Using a saucer or small plate as a guide, cut out four 5 inch (12 cm) circles from pastry. Transfer to a very large baking sheet (or 2 large baking sheets); prick pastry circles all over with a fork. Brush edges of circles with egg mixture. Repeat with second quarter of pastry.

Roll out third quarter of puff pastry to an 11 inch (28 cm) square. Using same saucer or plate as a guide, cut out 4 more circles from pastry. With a 3-1/2 inch (9 cm) cookie cutter, cut a hole in centre of each of these pastry circles. Place on 4 of the original circles to form a border. Repeat with final quarter of puff pastry to make borders for the remaining 4 pastry circles. Refrigerate for 30 minutes.

Preheat the oven to 400°F (200°C). With sharp kitchen scissors, cut tiny triangles out of edges of pastries so they resemble "sun" shapes. Brush edges of pastries with egg mixture. Spoon 2 tbsp (25 mL) almond cream onto each pastry, spreading to cover centre. Cover pastries with a sheet of parchment paper; bake for 15 to 18 minutes until pastries are golden brown and crisp, switching position of baking sheets halfway through cooking time if using 2 sheets. Remove pastries to a wire rack to cool completely. Leave oven on.

In a large bowl, gently toss peaches with icing sugar. Arrange peaches on a large parchment-paper-lined baking sheet; bake for 8 to 10 minutes, turning once, until golden and tender. Let cool on baking sheet.

Just before serving, top each pastry with 2 tbsp (25 mL) pastry cream, spreading to cover almond filling. Arrange 8 peach wedges cut sides up and resembling the rays of the sun on top of each pastry, leaving a space in the centre. Spoon a scoop of basil sorbet in centre of each pastry. Garnish with basil leaves.
Makes 8 servings

Laurent Pillard, executive chef of Fleur de Lys Las Vegas, was a guest chef at the Granite Club in 2006 and created the fabulous basil sorbet that garnishes this pretty dessert. Look for almond flour in the health food section of your supermarket and store in the freezer after opening. Most bulk stores sell glucose syrup.

PEAR ROULADE & MAPLE ICE CREAM

Maple Ice Cream:

5 egg yolks

1/3 cup (75 mL) sugar

1 cup (250 mL) homogenized (3.25%) milk

1 cup (250 mL) whipping cream

1 cup (250 mL) maple syrup

1 cinnamon stick, broken in half

Pear Roulade:

4 cups (1 L) water

2-1/4 cups (550 mL) sugar

2 lemon slices

2 cloves

1 cinnamon stick, broken in half

4 ripe pears (2 lb/1 kg), peeled, cored and each sliced lengthwise into 8 wedges

1/2 tsp (2 mL) ground cinnamon

8 sheets frozen phyllo pastry, thawed according to package directions

3/4 cup (175 mL) butter, clarified (page 18)

2 tbsp (25 mL) sliced almonds

Icing sugar

Crisp shortbread wafers

Mint sprigs

Maple Ice Cream: In a medium bowl, beat egg yolks. Add sugar; beat for 2 minutes until thick and pale. In a medium saucepan, combine milk, cream, maple syrup and cinnamon stick; bring to a simmer over medium-high heat. Whisk one-third of milk mixture into egg yolk mixture; return yolk mixture to saucepan. Cook over medium-low heat for 2 to 3 minutes, whisking constantly, until custard loses its raw egg taste (do not boil). Remove from heat; strain through a fine sieve into a medium bowl. Return cinnamon stick to bowl. Let cool to room temperature; whisk well until smooth. Lay a piece of plastic wrap directly on surface of custard; chill well. Discard cinnamon stick.

Pour custard into an ice cream maker and churn according to manufacturer's instructions. Alternatively, pour custard into a shallow 6 cup (1.5 L) container (preferably metal); freeze, covered, for 2 to 3 hours until a 1 inch (2.5 cm) frozen border has formed around edge. Scrape ice cream into a food processor; pulse until smooth. Scrape back into container. Repeat freezing and processing step once more; freeze, covered, for at least 3 hours until firm.

Pear Roulade: In a large saucepan, stir together water, 2 cups (500 mL) sugar, the lemon slices, cloves and cinnamon stick; bring to a boil over high heat. Add pears. Reduce heat to medium-low. Cover with a piece of parchment paper laid directly on pears; simmer, uncovered, for 5 minutes or until pears are tender but not broken up. With a slotted spoon, remove pears to a colander, discarding flavourings; let cool completely.

Preheat the oven to 375°F (190°C). In a medium bowl, stir together remaining sugar and the cinnamon; set aside 1 tsp (5 mL) cinnamon sugar in a small bowl. Add pears to sugar mixture in medium bowl; toss gently to coat well.

Lay 1 sheet of phyllo on work surface with 1 long end toward you; brush with clarified butter. Top with second sheet of phyllo; brush with more clarified butter. Repeat with remaining phyllo and butter, making a stack of 8 sheets of phyllo, reserving about 1 tbsp (15 mL) butter for brushing tops of roulades. Cut phyllo in half vertically to make 2 even-size pieces.

Using a slotted spoon, arrange half of pears lengthwise down centre of each phyllo rectangle; fold 1 long side of dough over each portion of pears; roll carefully to enclose filling, forming 2 roulades. Carefully transfer to a large parchment-paper-lined baking sheet, placing roulades seam side down. Brush each roulade with remaining butter; sprinkle evenly with almonds and reserved cinnamon sugar. Bake for 30 to 40 minutes until pastry is golden brown. Cut each roulade crosswise into 3 even-size pieces; dust with icing sugar. Arrange 1 slice on each of 6 plates; serve with maple ice cream. Garnish with shortbread wafers and mint.
Makes 6 servings

This fabulous dessert featuring juicy pears and crisp phyllo can be served warm or at room temperature.

Butternut Squash & Red Beet Soup (recipe on page 158)

OCTOBER
NOVEMBER
DECEMBER

Autumn fills me with inspiration. Such a time of contrasts — the warm

sun of day and the refreshing coolness of night. Nature puts on her

most colourful attire. The woods are filled with vermilion and orange

flounces. Soon she will shed her spectacular colours and dress in

winter white with icy trim. I am digging in with the spirit of the thing.

I feel a creative rush with the last harvest and thrill to winter's

possibilities. This cuisine requires a special kind of alchemy.

GIVING THANKS

The Thanksgiving Feast — roast turkey, Grandma's stuffing, a medley of beautiful and flavourful vegetables, rich and creamy potatoes and yams — such reassuring familiarity. The fabulous abundance of nature, the celebration of plenty. Each family has its own repertoire of old favourites, but I rather like the idea of giving the traditional feast a dashing little twist. One of my favourite soups, butternut squash, a classic puréed soup, treats the palate with a creamy, silky texture and then an explosion of the vegetable's natural flavour. And for the grand finale, a tasty pumpkin pie.

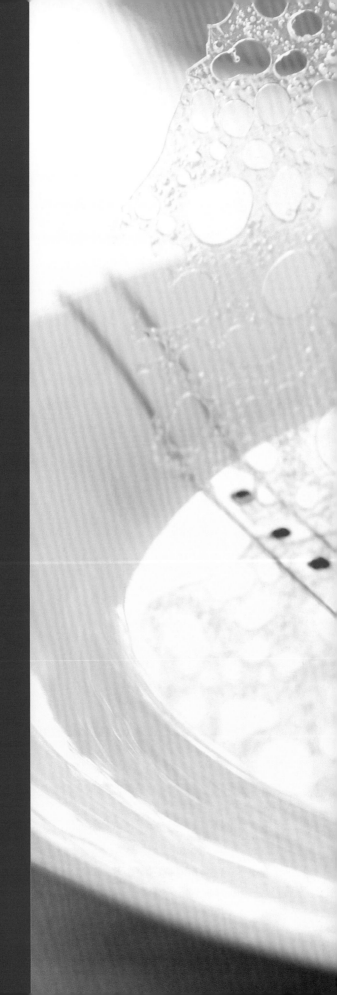

BUTTERNUT SQUASH & RED BEET SOUP

with Garlic Chips

Butternut Squash Soup:
1 large butternut squash (3 lb/1.5 kg), peeled, seeded and cut into 1/2 inch (1 cm) pieces

1/4 cup (50 mL) maple syrup

Salt and pepper

2 tbsp (25 mL) butter

1 onion, chopped

1 stalk celery, chopped

5 cups (1.2 L) Chicken Stock (page 217)

Red Beet Soup:
4 medium red beets (1 lb 12 oz/875 g)

2 tbsp (25 mL) balsamic vinegar

1 tsp (5 mL) liquid honey

2 cups (500 mL) Chicken Stock (page 217)

Salt and pepper

Garlic Chips:
1 cup (250 mL) canola oil

4 cloves garlic, very thinly sliced lengthwise

Table salt

Crème Fraîche (page 217)

Chervil

Butternut Squash Soup: Preheat the oven to 400°F (200°C). In a large bowl, toss together squash, maple syrup, and salt and pepper to taste. Spread out on a large parchment-paper-lined, rimmed baking sheet; roast for 25 to 30 minutes, stirring once or twice, until squash is tender and just starting to brown.

In a large pot or Dutch oven, melt butter over medium heat. Add onion and celery; cook for 3 to 5 minutes, stirring often, until onion is softened but not brown. Stir in squash and stock; bring to a boil over high heat. Reduce heat to low; simmer, covered, for 25 to 30 minutes until celery is tender. Remove from heat.

In a blender (not a food processor), blend soup in batches until smooth. Rub through a fine sieve into rinsed-out pot, discarding solids in sieve. If soup is too thick, add a little more chicken stock. Season with more salt and pepper to taste. Set aside.

Red Beet Soup: Preheat the oven to 400°F (200°C). Scrub beets gently; trim off roots and all but 1/2 inch (1 cm) of stems. Wrap each beet individually in foil; roast for 1 to 1-1/2 hours (depending on size) until beets feel tender when pierced with a slim knife.

Remove beets from the oven; remove foil and set beets aside until cool enough to handle. Trim off remaining stems; remove skin with your fingers. Cut each beet into 8 wedges. In a large, non-reactive bowl, toss beets with vinegar and honey. Set aside to marinate until cooled to room temperature.

In a large saucepan, stir together beets and chicken stock; bring to a boil over high heat. Reduce heat to low; simmer, covered, for 10 minutes for flavours to blend. Remove from heat; let cool slightly.

In a blender (not a food processor), blend soup in batches until smooth. Rub through a fine sieve into rinsed-out saucepan, discarding solids in sieve. If soup is too thick, add a little more chicken stock. Season with salt and pepper to taste. Set aside.

Garlic Chips: In a small skillet, heat oil until a candy thermometer registers 325°F (160°C). Cook garlic chips in hot oil for 30 seconds, stirring occasionally, until golden and crisp. Remove with a slotted spoon; drain on a paper-towel-lined plate. Sprinkle with salt to taste.

Reheat both soups separately. Ladle butternut squash soup into 6 soup bowls, dividing evenly. Using a clean ladle, ladle red beet soup in centre of each bowl; swirl decoratively with a slim knife. Garnish each portion with crème fraîche, chervil and garlic chips.

Makes 6 servings

This stunning bi-coloured winter soup is very hearty so serve it before a light main course.

RICH PUMPKIN PIES

with Hazelnut Ice Cream & Vanilla Mousseline

Hazelnut Ice Cream:
4 egg yolks
1/2 cup (125 mL) sugar
1 vanilla bean
1 cup (250 mL) homogenized (3.25%) milk
1 cup (250 mL) whipping cream
Pinch salt
1/2 cup (125 mL) hazelnut paste
(see note below)

Sugar Pastry:
1-1/4 cups (300 mL) flour
1 tbsp (15 mL) sugar
Pinch table salt
1/2 cup (125 mL) cold butter, cubed
1 egg, lightly beaten

Pumpkin Filling:
3/4 cup (175 mL) fresh or canned pumpkin purée
(not pie filling)
1/4 cup (50 mL) sugar
1/4 cup (50 mL) packed light brown sugar
1/4 cup (50 mL) whipping cream
1 egg
1 tbsp (15 mL) brandy or whisky (optional)
1/2 tsp (2 mL) ground cinnamon
1/4 tsp (1 mL) ground allspice
1/4 tsp (1 mL) ground ginger
Pinch ground cloves
Pinch grated nutmeg

Vanilla Mousseline:
Pastry Cream (page 217)
1 cup (250 mL) whipping cream
Mint sprigs
Chocolate shards

Hazelnut Ice Cream: In a medium bowl, beat egg yolks. Add sugar; beat for 2 minutes until thick and pale. With a small knife, split vanilla bean lengthwise; scrape seeds from bean. In a medium saucepan, combine vanilla bean and its seeds, the milk, cream and salt; bring to a simmer over medium-high heat. Whisk one-third of milk mixture into egg yolk mixture; return yolk mixture to saucepan. Cook over medium-low heat for 2 to 3 minutes, whisking constantly, until custard loses its raw egg taste (do not boil). Remove from heat; strain through a fine sieve into a medium bowl. Whisk in hazelnut paste until smooth. Add vanilla bean back into custard. Let cool to room temperature; whisk well until smooth. Lay a piece of plastic wrap directly on surface of custard; chill well. Discard vanilla bean.

Pour custard into an ice cream maker and churn according to manufacturer's instructions. Alternatively, pour custard into a shallow 6 cup (1.5 L) container (preferably metal); freeze, covered, for 2 to 3 hours until a 1 inch (2.5 cm) frozen border has formed around edge. Scrape ice cream into a food processor; pulse until smooth and creamy. Scrape back into container. Repeat freezing and processing step once more; freeze, covered, for at least 3 hours until firm.

Sugar Pastry: In a food processor, pulse flour, sugar and salt until combined. Add butter; pulse until mixture resembles coarse crumbs. With motor running, add egg through feed tube; process just until dough clumps together. Turn out onto a floured surface. Gather dough into a ball; wrap in plastic wrap. Refrigerate for 20 minutes.

Grease six 4 inch (10 cm) individual tart pans well. Divide pastry into 6 pieces; form into balls. With your thumbs, press a ball of pastry over base and up sides of each tart pan to line neatly, making sure to press pastry into corners and fluted sides. Trim off any excess pastry from each tart pan. Prick pastry all over with a fork. Put tart pans on a baking sheet; refrigerate for 1 hour.

Preheat the oven to 375°F (190°C). Line each tart with a piece of foil; fill with pie weights or dried beans. Bake for 15 minutes until edges of pastry are very pale gold. Remove foil and pie weights; set aside. Leave oven on.

Pumpkin Filling: While pastry is baking, in a medium bowl and using an electric mixer, beat pumpkin purée, sugar, brown sugar, cream, egg, brandy, cinnamon, allspice, ginger, cloves and nutmeg until smooth and well combined. Pour filling into hot tart shells, dividing evenly; bake for 20 to 25 minutes until filling is just set around edges but still jiggles in the centre, and pastry is golden. Remove to a wire rack; let cool completely.

Vanilla Mousseline: Spoon pastry cream into a medium bowl. In a separate medium bowl, whip cream until soft peaks form. Stir one-quarter of whipped cream into pastry cream to lighten it; gradually fold in remaining whipped cream until well combined and no white streaks remain.

To serve, carefully loosen edges of tarts; remove from pans. Put 1 tart on each of 6 plates. Top each with a scoop of hazelnut ice cream; garnish plates with vanilla mousseline, mint sprigs and chocolate shards.
Makes 6 servings

Hazelnut paste is a sweet amalgam of nuts, sugar and vanilla that provides an easy way to add rich flavour to ice creams and mousses. Order it on-line from www.bernardcallebaut.com.

ESCAROLE, FRISÉE & ENDIVE SALAD

with Smoked Duck

1/2 cup (125 mL) hazelnuts

3 tbsp (45 mL) red wine vinegar

2 tbsp (25 mL) finely diced shallots

2 tsp (10 mL) Dijon mustard

Salt and pepper

1/2 cup (125 mL) hazelnut oil

3 cups (750 mL) lightly packed, washed, dried and torn escarole

3 cups (750 mL) lightly packed, washed, dried and torn frisée

2 Belgian endive, trimmed, cored and torn

5 oz (150 g) Gruyère cheese, cut into 1/2 inch (1 cm) cubes and rind discarded (about 1 cup/250 mL cubes)

1 smoked boneless duck magret (about 14 oz/425 g), thinly sliced, skin and fat discarded

Chervil

Chives

Preheat the oven to 350°F (180°C). Spread hazelnuts out on a rimmed baking sheet; bake for 6 to 8 minutes, shaking baking sheet occasionally, until nuts are golden brown and fragrant. Enclose hazelnuts in a clean towel; rub vigorously to remove any loose skins. Chop nuts coarsely; let cool completely.

In a large salad bowl, whisk together vinegar, shallots, mustard, and salt and pepper to taste. Gradually whisk in oil until dressing is smooth and creamy.

Just before serving, whisk dressing again. Add escarole, frisée and Belgian endive; toss well. Add cheese and hazelnuts; toss again. Spoon salad onto 6 plates, dividing evenly. Arrange smoked duck breast on top of each portion. Garnish with chervil and chives.

Makes 6 servings

My lovely French wife, Catherine, who's a very talented cook, created this flavourful salad and I loved it so much I added it to the menu at the club. If you prefer, use prosciutto in place of smoked duck.

CHOCOLATE

When I was young, I loved chocolate: Gooey chocolate licked from my fingers and the cooking spoon — my version of cleanup in Grandmother's kitchen — or rich, warm chocolate sauce poured over vanilla ice cream. As I've grown older, my chocolate desires have become more sophisticated. Now I look forward to the delicacy of a perfect soufflé or the creamy richness of a mousse. Oh, the seductive sweetness of chocolate tops almost everyone's list of favourites. Chocolate is so versatile — a flavouring ingredient, a warming, rich beverage, a delectable sauce or a crisp coating — all depending on how much cream you add. Dip fresh strawberries in soft melted chocolate, or pour a little over raspberries or a poached pear. It's precious, so many uses and each one gives pure enjoyment.

Individual Chocolate Souffles (recipe on page 166)

INDIVIDUAL CHOCOLATE SOUFFLÉS

5 oz (150 g) good-quality bittersweet
chocolate, finely chopped
3 tbsp (45 mL) flour
2 tbsp (25 mL) butter, softened
Pinch table salt
2/3 cup (150 mL) milk
2 tsp plus 3 tbsp (55 mL) sugar
1 tbsp (15 mL) cornstarch
3 eggs, separated
Icing sugar

Preheat the oven to 375°F (190°C). Lightly butter six 2/3 cup (150 mL) individual soufflé dishes or straight-sided ramekins; sprinkle lightly with sugar, shaking out excess. Put dishes in a shallow roasting pan.

Put chocolate in a medium bowl. In a large bowl, blend flour, butter and salt together until a smooth, creamy paste forms. In a small saucepan, whisk together milk, 2 tsp (10 mL) sugar and the cornstarch until smooth. Bring to a boil over medium-high heat, stirring constantly. Pour over chocolate. Let stand 1 minute to soften chocolate; whisk well until smooth.

Add chocolate mixture to flour mixture, whisking well until smooth; whisk in egg yolks 1 at a time, whisking well after each addition.

In a separate bowl, beat egg whites until soft peaks form. Sprinkle remaining sugar over egg whites; beat until stiff peaks form. Blend one-quarter of egg whites into chocolate mixture to lighten it, then gradually fold in remaining egg whites until well combined and no white streaks remain.

Spoon soufflé mixture into prepared dishes, dividing evenly. Pour boiling water into roasting pan to come halfway up sides of dishes. Bake for 15 to 20 minutes until well risen and puffy. Dust with icing sugar; serve at once.
Makes 6 servings

Light as air but sinfully rich, these cute desserts need a little last-minute attention and, like all soufflés, wait for no-one but they're easy to prepare and make a great finale to a special dinner.

DECADENT CHOCOLATE MOUSSE

4 large eggs, separated
1/2 cup plus 1 tbsp (140 mL) sugar
2 tbsp (25 mL) Cognac or brandy
8 oz (250 g) good-quality bittersweet
chocolate, chopped
1/2 cup (125 mL) butter, softened
Pinch table salt
Whipped cream and fresh berries

In a medium heatproof bowl, stir together egg yolks, 1/2 cup (125 mL) sugar and the Cognac. Set the bowl over a saucepan of hot, not boiling, water, making sure base of bowl doesn't touch the water. Using an electric mixer, beat egg yolk mixture for 4 minutes or until thick and pale yellow. Remove bowl from heat and set aside, leaving saucepan on burner.

Set a second medium heatproof bowl over the saucepan of hot water. Put chocolate in bowl; allow to melt until almost smooth. Remove bowl from heat; stir chocolate until smooth. Using electric mixer, beat butter into chocolate a little at a time, until mixture is smooth and glossy; set aside.

Wash beaters well. In a separate medium bowl and using electric mixer, beat egg whites and salt until soft peaks form. Sprinkle remaining sugar over egg whites; beat until stiff peaks form.

Stir melted chocolate into egg yolk mixture until well combined. Blend one-quarter of egg whites into chocolate mixture to lighten it, then gradually fold in remaining egg whites until well combined and no white streaks remain. Spoon mousse into 6 or 8 glasses or serving dishes, dividing evenly. Refrigerate, covered, for at least 2 hours or overnight. Garnish with whipped cream and fresh berries.
Makes 6 to 8 servings

Valrhona or Lindt chocolate are best for this rich mousse but if those brands aren't available, choose one that contains a minimum of 50% cocoa solids (check the label) so the mousse tastes as chocolatey as it looks.

SILKEN CHOCOLATE TART

Tart Pastry:
2/3 cup (150 mL) icing sugar
1/2 cup (125 mL) butter, softened
2 egg yolks
1-1/2 cups (375 mL) flour
1 tbsp (15 mL) cold water

Filling:
12 oz (375 g) good-quality bittersweet
chocolate, chopped
2 eggs
2/3 cup (150 mL) milk
2/3 cup (150 mL) whipping cream
Chocolate shavings
Chocolate syrup

Tart Pastry: In a medium bowl and using an electric mixer, beat icing sugar and butter until fluffy and pale. Add egg yolks one at a time, beating well after each addition. Add flour and water; beat for 1 to 2 minutes until smooth. Scrape dough onto a sheet of plastic wrap. Pat into a disc; wrap tightly then refrigerate for 1 hour.

On a lightly floured surface, roll out dough to 1/4 inch (5 mm) thickness. Carefully transfer pastry to a lightly greased 9 inch (23 cm) tart pan with a removeable base, fitting it gently into pan to line neatly and pressing into the corners and fluted sides. Trim off excess pastry, using trimmings to patch pastry if necessary. Prick pastry with a fork. Set tart pan on a large plate; refrigerate for 1 hour.

Preheat the oven to 350°F (180°C). Set tart pan on a baking sheet. Line tart shell with foil and fill with pie weights or dried beans; bake for 15 minutes or until edges of pastry are golden and centre looks dry. Remove foil and pie weights; bake for 5 minutes until pastry is golden. Let cool completely on a wire rack.

Filling: Preheat the oven to 375°F (190°C). Put chocolate in a medium heatproof bowl. Set the bowl over a saucepan of hot, not boiling, water, making sure base of bowl doesn't touch the water; allow chocolate to melt until almost smooth. Remove bowl from heat; stir chocolate until smooth. Set aside.

In a separate bowl, whisk eggs. In a small saucepan, bring milk and cream to a boil over medium-high heat. Pour milk mixture over eggs, whisking well. Strain milk mixture through a sieve into bowl containing chocolate; whisk until smooth and well combined. Pour chocolate mixture into baked tart shell.

Put tart in oven; immediately turn the oven off. Leave tart in oven, without opening the door, for 45 minutes until filling is just set. Let tart cool completely on a wire rack. Carefully loosen edges of tart; remove sides of pan. Cut tart into wedges; put wedges on dessert plates. Garnish tart with chocolate shavings and drizzle plates with chocolate syrup.
Makes 10 to 12 servings

This ultra-rich tart is best served in slim slices and at room temperature. It does keep well in the refrigerator for up to 3 days but let it sit at room temperature for approximately 1 hour before serving. We garnished it with chocolate shavings and chocolate syrup but whipped cream or vanilla ice cream are also decadent additions.

GRANITE BALL

There are high spirits in the kitchen, a hustle and bustle since

morning. The rhythm and tempo increase as the evening of the Granite

Ball approaches. You can sense the anticipation. The cuisine must be

exemplary and the service invisible and impeccable. The moment is

here — the first guests are arriving in all their splendour, ready to

enjoy their special night in every way. We are all on stage and each

one of us will play a flawless part. This is a magical time. The music

begins to pulsate through the rooms, at first melodious then a

throbbing beat. The remarkable Granite Ball is in full swing.

PEPPERED SMOKED SALMON

with Bagel Chips, Avocado Salsa & Potted Crab

Potted Crab:

1 live Dungeness crab (about 2 lb/1 kg)

16 cups (4 L) Court Bouillon (page 216)

1 cup (250 mL) butter

1 small carrot, coarsely chopped

Half stalk celery, coarsely chopped

3 tbsp (45 mL) coarsely chopped shallots

2 cloves garlic, halved

1 sprig rosemary

1 sprig thyme

1 small plum tomato, coarsely chopped

Pinch crumbled saffron

Salt and pepper

2 tbsp (25 mL) chopped tarragon

Avocado Salsa:

2 avocados

1/4 cup (50 mL) lemon juice

2 medium tomatoes, peeled, cored,

seeded and diced

2 tbsp (25 mL) finely chopped chives

2 tbsp (25 mL) finely chopped tarragon

Salt and pepper

8 oz (250 g) thinly sliced peppered smoked salmon

Frisée

6 bagel chips

Fennel fronds

Potted Crab: Cook crab in a large pot of court bouillon and remove meat from shells as described on page 115, reserving shells. Chop meat finely; refrigerate shells and meat separately.

Preheat the oven to 300°F (150°C). In a large, deep pot or large, sturdy metal bowl, pound crab shells with the end of a wooden rolling pin until finely crushed; set aside.

In a medium, flameproof casserole dish, heat 1 tbsp (15 mL) butter over medium heat. Add carrot, celery, shallots, garlic, rosemary and thyme; cook, stirring often, for 5 to 7 minutes until shallots are soft but not browned. Stir in tomato. Reduce heat to medium-low; cook, covered, for 6 to 8 minutes until tomato starts to soften. Do not let vegetables brown. Increase heat to medium; stir in reserved crab shells and saffron. Cook, stirring occasionally, for 2 to 3 minutes until fragrant.

Cut remaining butter into cubes; add to casserole, poking it down among ingredients. Cover dish; transfer to the oven. Bake for 30 minutes until butter has melted and flavours are blended. Remove from the oven; let stand for 1 hour. Strain contents of casserole through a fine sieve into a medium bowl, discarding solids. Season with salt and pepper to taste. Refrigerate, covered, for at least 1 hour until butter has solidified.

Set six 1/3 cup (75 mL) cone-shaped paper cups (like the ones dispensed at water coolers) in 6 narrow drinking glasses. In a medium bowl, stir together crab meat and tarragon. Remove solidified butter from bowl, discarding any liquid underneath. In a small saucepan, melt solidified butter over medium heat. Carefully pour butter over crab meat, leaving any milky residue in saucepan; stir crab mixture to combine. Season with salt and pepper to taste.

Working quickly, spoon crab mixture into paper cups, dividing evenly and pressing mixture down firmly in each one. Refrigerate for at least 1 hour until set.

Avocado Salsa: Just before serving, cut avocados in half; remove pits. With a 1/2 inch (1 cm) melon baller, scoop balls from 1 avocado. In a small bowl, toss avocado balls with 1 tbsp (15 mL) lemon juice to coat completely. Remove peel from remaining avocado; cut into 1/2 inch (1 cm) cubes. In a medium bowl, stir together cubed avocado, remaining lemon juice, tomatoes, chives, tarragon, and salt and pepper to taste.

To serve, divide smoked salmon among 6 plates. Set a 2 inch (5 cm) metal ring or cookie cutter on top of one portion of salmon. With a slotted spoon, spoon one-sixth of avocado salsa into ring. Gently push salsa onto plate, removing ring. Repeat with remaining salsa and plates. Top salsa with frisée. Peel paper cups from potted crab; set 1 potted crab pyramid on top of each portion of frisée and top with bagel chips. Drain reserved avocado balls; garnish with avocado balls and fennel fronds.
Makes 6 servings

At the Granite Club we prepare our own smoked salmon from scratch but to make this recipe at home it's easier if you buy good-quality cold-smoked salmon. Similarly, we make our own bagel chips by thinly slicing frozen bagels on a meat slicer then toasting them until crisp, but good-quality bagel chips from a specialty food store would work just as well. Follow the instructions for cooking a crab and removing its meat in the recipe for Dungeness Crab Cakes on page 115.

ROASTED BEEF TENDERLOIN

& Braised Short Ribs with Candied Sweet Potato & Bok Choy Confit

Braised Short Ribs:
1 cup (250 mL) red wine
1 medium carrot, finely chopped
1 stalk celery, finely chopped
1 small onion, finely chopped
2 cloves garlic, crushed
1 sprig rosemary
1 sprig thyme
4 pieces beef short ribs (about 1-1/2 lb/750 g)
Salt and pepper
1 tbsp (15 mL) butter
1 tbsp (15 mL) olive oil
1 tsp (5 mL) tomato paste
1 cup (250 mL) Beef or Veal Stock (page 216)

Bok Choy Confit:
1/2 cup (125 mL) Chicken Stock (page 217)
2 tbsp (25 mL) butter
Salt and pepper
2 baby bok choy (8 oz/250 g),
halved lengthwise

Candied Sweet Potato:
1 medium sweet potato (12 oz/375 g)
Salt
1 tbsp (15 mL) butter
1 tsp (5 mL) liquid honey
Pepper

Roasted Beef Tenderloin:
1/2 tsp (2 mL) minced garlic
1/2 tsp (2 mL) finely chopped rosemary
1/2 tsp (2 mL) finely chopped thyme
4 pieces beef tenderloin (4 oz/125 g each)
Salt and pepper
1 tbsp (15 mL) butter
1 tsp (5 mL) olive oil

Braised Short Ribs: In a large, non-reactive bowl, stir together wine, carrot, celery, onion, garlic, rosemary and thyme. Add short ribs, turning to coat well; refrigerate, covered, for 48 hours, turning occasionally.

Preheat the oven to 325°F (160°C). Remove ribs from marinade, scraping vegetables and herbs back into marinade and reserving marinade. Strain marinade, reserving vegetables and liquid separately. Pat ribs dry; sprinkle with salt and pepper to taste. In a large flameproof casserole or Dutch oven, heat butter and oil over medium-high heat. Sear ribs in batches for 3 minutes, turning often, until browned on all sides and removing ribs to a plate as each batch browns. Add vegetables and herbs from marinade to pot; cook for 3 to 5 minutes, stirring often, until vegetables start to brown. Stir in tomato paste; cook, stirring, for 1 minute. Stir in liquid from marinade; bring to a boil, stirring to scrape up any browned bits from bottom of pot. Reduce heat to medium; boil for 2 to 3 minutes until liquid has reduced to 2 tbsp (25 mL). Stir in stock; bring to a boil. Season with salt and pepper to taste. Return short ribs to pot, along with any juices that have accumulated on plate. Cover tightly; bake for 2 hours until meat is tender and falling off the bones.

With a slotted spoon, remove ribs to a plate; cover and keep warm. Bring contents of pot to a boil over high heat; boil for 3 to 5 minutes, stirring occasionally, until liquid has reduced to 1 cup (250 mL) and is thick enough to coat the back of a spoon. Season with salt and pepper to taste. Return short ribs to pot; keep warm.

Bok Choy Confit: In a shallow, medium saucepan, combine chicken stock, butter, and salt and pepper to taste. Bring to a boil over high heat; add bok choy. Reduce heat to medium; simmer, uncovered, for 6 to 8 minutes, turning bok choy occasionally, until tender. Increase heat to high; boil for 2 minutes until liquid has reduced and is syrupy. Keep warm.

Candied Sweet Potato: Peel potato; cut into six 1/2 inch (1 cm) slices, reserving remaining potato for use in another recipe. Cut each slice in half to make 12 semi-circles. With a 3 inch (8 cm) cookie cutter, cut a piece out of straight side of each semi-circle to make a crescent moon shape, discarding trimmings. In a small saucepan of boiling, salted water, cook slices for 3 minutes until tender-crisp; drain well. Spread out on a clean towel to dry.

In a medium, good-quality non-stick skillet, heat butter and honey over medium heat. Add sweet potato slices; cook for 6 to 8 minutes, turning often, until tender and golden. Season with salt and pepper; keep warm.

Roasted Beef Tenderloin: Preheat the oven to 400°F (200°C). In a small bowl, stir together garlic, rosemary and thyme; rub all over both sides of beef tenderloin pieces. Sprinkle on both sides with salt and pepper. In a large, ovenproof skillet, heat butter and olive oil over medium-high heat. Add beef tenderloin; sear for 1 to 2 minutes, turning once, until golden brown on both sides. Transfer skillet to oven; cook for 4 to 5 minutes for medium-rare. Remove to a cutting board; tent with foil and let stand for 5 minutes.

Place a piece of bok choy on each of 4 plates; top each with a piece of beef tenderloin. Lean a portion of short ribs next to tenderloin; drizzle reduced braising liquid around plates, discarding herb sprigs. Garnish with candied sweet potatoes.
Makes 4 servings

Start this recipe 2 days ahead to allow plenty of time for the short ribs to marinate.

CHOCOLATE CARRÉ

with Hazelnut Mousse & Black Pepper Ice Cream

Black Pepper Ice Cream:

2 tsp (10 mL) black peppercorns

4 oz (125 g) good-quality semi-sweet chocolate, finely chopped

4 egg yolks

1/2 cup (125 mL) sugar

1 cup (250 mL) homogenized (3.25%) milk

1 cup (250 mL) whipping cream

1 tbsp (15 mL) liquid honey

1 cinnamon stick, broken in half

2/3 cup (150 mL) sifted unsweetened cocoa powder

Orange-Sesame Tuiles:

1/2 cup (125 mL) sugar

1/3 cup (75 mL) flour

1/3 cup (75 mL) sesame seeds

1/4 cup (50 mL) butter, melted

3 tbsp (45 mL) orange juice

2 tsp (10 mL) grated orange rind

Hazelnut Mousse:

4 egg yolks

2 tbsp (25 mL) sugar

2 tsp (10 mL) unflavoured powdered gelatine

1/3 cup (75 mL) hazelnut paste (see note page 159)

2/3 cup (150 mL) whipping cream

1/2 tsp (2 mL) vanilla

Black Pepper Ice Cream: In a small, dry skillet, toast peppercorns over medium heat for 3 minutes until fragrant. Let cool slightly. In a clean spice or coffee grinder, grind peppercorns finely; set aside. Put chocolate in a medium bowl; set aside.

In a separate medium bowl, beat egg yolks. Add sugar; beat for 2 minutes until thick and pale. In a medium saucepan, combine milk, cream, honey and cinnamon stick; bring to a simmer over medium-high heat. Whisk one-third of milk mixture into egg yolk mixture; return yolk mixture to saucepan. Cook over medium-low heat for 2 to 3 minutes, whisking constantly, until custard loses its raw egg taste (do not boil). Remove from heat; strain through a fine sieve into bowl of chocolate. Sprinkle cocoa powder over surface; let stand 1 minute to soften chocolate. Whisk well until smooth. Let cool to room temperature; whisk well until smooth. Stir in black pepper. Lay a piece of plastic wrap directly on surface of custard; chill well.

Pour custard into an ice cream maker and churn according to manufacturer's instructions. Alternatively, pour custard into a shallow 6 cup (1.5 L) container (preferably metal); freeze, covered, for 2 to 3 hours until a 1 inch (2.5 cm) frozen border has formed around edge. Scrape ice cream into a food processor; pulse until smooth and creamy. Scrape back into container. Repeat freezing and processing step once more; freeze, covered, for at least 3 hours until firm.

Orange-Sesame Tuiles: In a medium bowl, whisk together sugar, flour and sesame seeds. In a small bowl, stir together butter and orange juice; stir into sugar mixture until smooth. Stir in orange rind. Refrigerate, covered, for 1 to 2 hours until thick enough to spread. If batter is refrigerated for longer, let stand at room temperature for 1 hour until spreadable.

Preheat the oven to 350°F (180°C). Using a pencil, draw four 3 inch (8 cm) star or flower shapes or circles well apart on a large piece of parchment paper. Turn paper over so pencil marks are on underside; use to line a large baking sheet. Using 2 tbsp (25 mL) batter for each tuile, spoon tuile batter onto shapes, spreading to just inside pencil lines. Bake for 10 to 12 minutes until golden around edges and lacy in the centre. Let cool on baking sheet for 5 minutes; remove carefully with a spatula and let cool completely on a wire rack. Repeat with remaining batter. Store in an airtight container until ready to serve.

Hazelnut Mousse: In a medium heatproof bowl and using a hand-held electric mixer, beat egg yolks and sugar until frothy. Set bowl over a saucepan of simmering water; cook, beating constantly with electric mixer, for 4 minutes until mixture is the consistency of softly whipped cream. Remove bowl from heat; let cool to room temperature.

Meanwhile, pour 2 tbsp (25 mL) cold water into a small bowl; sprinkle gelatine over surface. Let stand for 5 minutes until puffy; put bowl in a saucepan containing enough barely simmering water to come halfway up side of bowl. Heat, stirring often, for 1 minute or until gelatine has completely dissolved.

Beat hazelnut paste into egg mixture until well combined; beat in gelatine. In a medium bowl, whip cream and vanilla until soft peaks form; fold whipped cream into hazelnut mixture until well combined and no white streaks remain. Refrigerate, covered, for at least 2 hours or until ready to serve.

Poached Pears:

1/4 cup (50 mL) lemon juice

4 firm, ripe Comice pears (1-1/2 lb/750 g)

1-1/2 cups (375 mL) white wine

1 cup (250 mL) water

1 cup (250 mL) sugar

2 cinnamon sticks, broken in half

1 vanilla bean, split

1 star anise

Chocolate Carré:

6 oz (175 g) good-quality semi-sweet or
bittersweet chocolate, chopped

1/3 cup (75 mL) butter

4 eggs, separated

1/3 cup (75 mL) sugar

Ganache:

4 oz (125 g) good-quality semi-sweet
chocolate, finely chopped

1/2 cup (125 mL) whipping cream

Poached Pears: Put lemon juice in a medium bowl. Cut pears in half; remove cores with a melon baller. Cut out tough stems and blossom ends. Peel pear halves, dropping each 1 into bowl of lemon juice as you work, tossing well to coat with juice.

In a large, non-reactive saucepan, stir together wine, water, sugar, cinnamon sticks, vanilla bean and star anise; bring to a boil over high heat. Drain pear halves, discarding lemon juice; add pear halves to saucepan. Reduce heat to medium-low. Cover with a piece of parchment paper laid directly on pears; simmer, uncovered, for 20 to 25 minutes until pears are tender but not broken up. Remove from heat; let cool completely. Pour pear halves and cooking liquid into a large, non-reactive bowl; refrigerate, covered, until ready to serve.

Chocolate Carré: Preheat the oven to 325°F (160°C). Butter an 8 inch (2 L) square baking pan; line base with parchment paper.

Put chocolate and butter in a large, heatproof bowl. Set the bowl over a saucepan of hot, not boiling, water, making sure base of bowl doesn't touch the water; allow chocolate to melt until almost smooth. Remove bowl from heat; stir until smooth. Set aside to cool to room temperature.

In a medium bowl, beat egg yolks and half of the sugar until thick and pale. Stir in one-quarter melted chocolate mixture. Stir egg mixture back into the remaining chocolate mixture.

In a separate bowl, beat egg whites until soft peaks form. Sprinkle remaining sugar over egg whites; beat until stiff peaks form. Stir one-quarter of egg whites into chocolate mixture to lighten it, then gradually fold in remaining egg whites until well combined and no white streaks remain. Pour batter into prepared pan; bake for 20 to 25 minutes until cake pulls away from sides of pan and centre springs back when touched gently. Let cool in pan for 5 minutes; turn out cake and let cool completely on a wire rack. Cake will sink slightly. Trim edges of cake neatly; cut cake into 8 even-size bars. Arrange well apart on a parchment-paper-lined baking sheet.

Ganache: Put chocolate in a medium bowl. In a small saucepan, bring cream to a boil over medium-high heat. Immediately, pour cream over chocolate; let stand for 1 minute to soften chocolate. Whisk well until smooth. Spread warm ganache over top and sides of each piece of cake; refrigerate for at least 30 minutes until set.

To serve, put a piece of cake on each of 8 plates; pipe a rosette of hazelnut mousse on 1 end of top of each piece. With a slotted spoon, remove pears from their poaching liquid; place 1 pear half on top of each piece of cake. Scoop ice cream onto each plate; garnish with tuiles.

Makes 8 servings

Comice pears are fragrant fruit with smooth, sweet flesh; if they're unavailable substitute Bartlett pears.

CHRISTMAS

Jingle bell weather has arrived. The first flakes of snow and the air is cold and crisp, a time for comfort and joy. Every year I like to create a Christmas dish that is unusual and unexpected, full of rich flavours that reflect the spirit of the holiday. This dish, coupled with a traditional favourite, gives surprise and familiarity — an intriguing pair. Let me share my family's old-time mincemeat pie recipe, it is absolutely delicious. The ingredients may be familiar, but wow! The crackers are pulled, the napkins unfurl, the wine is shared and as those gathered tuck in, the expressions on their faces are the most precious gifts of the season.

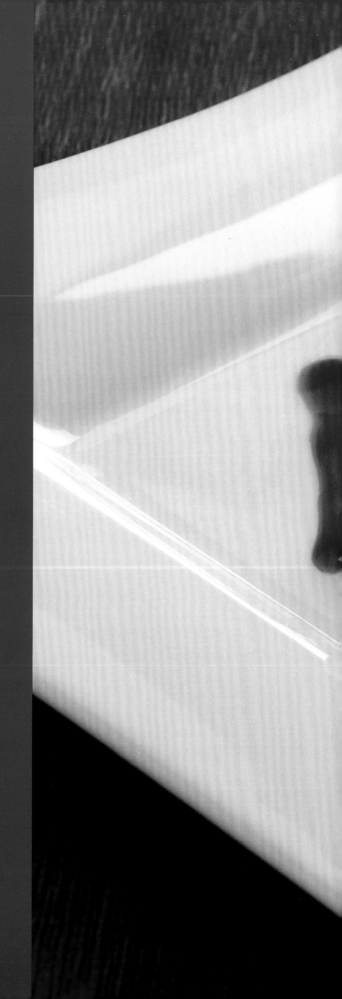

 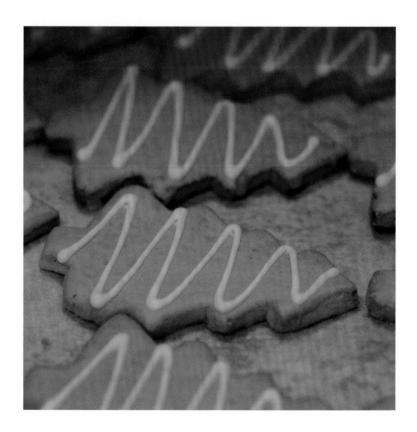

ROASTED VENISON LOIN

with Pumpkin Polenta, Pickled Pears & Sauce Grand Veneur

Sauce Grand Veneur:

1 piece venison loin (about 1-1/2 lb/750 g)
1 tbsp (15 mL) olive oil
1 carrot, coarsely chopped
1 stalk celery, coarsely chopped
2 tbsp (25 mL) coarsely chopped shallots
1 clove garlic, coarsely chopped
1/4 tsp (2 mL) black peppercorns
1 sprig thyme
1 bay leaf
1/4 cup (50 mL) red wine
1-1/2 tsp (7 mL) red currant jelly
2 cups (500 mL) Veal Stock (page 216)
2 tbsp (25 mL) whipping cream

Pickled Pears:

1 cup (250 mL) red wine vinegar
1/4 cup (50 mL) packed brown sugar
10 black peppercorns
1 sprig thyme
1 bay leaf
2 forelle pears (about 4 oz/125 g each), peeled,
cored and each cut into 6 wedges

Pumpkin Polenta:

1-1/2 cups (375 mL) Chicken Stock (page 217)
2 tbsp (25 mL) butter
1/2 cup (125 mL) quick-cooking polenta
1 cup (250 mL) fresh or canned unsweetened
pumpkin purée (not pie filling)
Salt and pepper

To Finish:

2 tbsp (25 mL) olive oil
Salt and pepper
One-quarter small pie pumpkin, peeled, seeded
and cut into 1/2 inch (1 cm) cubes
(about 1 cup/250 mL cubes)
Thyme sprigs

Sauce Grand Veneur: Trim venison loin of any visible fat. Cut crosswise into four 5 oz (150 g) pieces, reserving trimmings. Refrigerate veal pieces; chop trimmings.

In a medium saucepan, heat oil over medium-high heat. Add venison trimmings; cook, stirring, for 3 minutes until browned. Add carrot, celery, shallots, garlic, peppercorns, thyme and bay leaf. Reduce heat to medium; cook for 5 minutes, stirring often, until shallots start to soften. Stir in wine and jelly; increase heat to medium-high. Cook, stirring to scrape up any browned bits from bottom of saucepan, for 3 to 5 minutes until wine has almost all evaporated. Stir in veal stock; bring to a boil. Reduce the heat to medium; boil for 45 to 50 minutes until liquid has reduced to 3/4 cup (175 mL) and sauce is thick enough to coat the back of a spoon. Strain through a fine sieve into a clean saucepan; whisk in cream. Season with salt and pepper to taste; keep warm but do not boil.

Pickled Pears: In a medium, non-reactive saucepan, stir together vinegar, sugar, peppercorns, thyme and bay leaf; bring to a boil over medium-high heat. Add pears. Reduce heat to medium-low. Cover with a piece of parchment paper laid directly on pears; simmer, uncovered, for 5 minutes or until pears are tender but not broken up. With a slotted spoon, remove pears to a small, non-reactive bowl, leaving flavourings in saucepan.

Increase heat to medium-high; bring cooking liquid to a boil. Boil for 8 to 10 minutes until reduced to 2 tbsp (25 mL) and syrupy (watch carefully toward the end of cooking time to make sure liquid doesn't burn). Strain over pears; stir to coat well. Set aside.

Pumpkin Polenta: In a medium saucepan, stir together chicken stock and butter; bring to a boil over medium-high heat. Whisk in polenta until smooth. Reduce heat to low; cook, stirring constantly, for 3 minutes. Stir in pumpkin purée; cook for 1 to 2 minutes, stirring constantly. Season with salt and pepper; keep warm.

To Finish: Preheat the oven to 400°F (200°C). In a large ovenproof skillet, heat 1 tbsp (15 mL) oil over medium-high heat. Sprinkle venison pieces on both sides with salt and pepper to taste. Add venison to skillet; sear for 3 minutes, turning once, until golden brown on both sides. Transfer skillet to oven; cook for 5 to 6 minutes for medium-rare. Remove to a cutting board; tent loosely with foil and let rest for 5 minutes.

Meanwhile, in a medium skillet, heat remaining oil over medium heat. Add pumpkin; cook, stirring often, for 6 to 8 minutes until golden and tender. Season with salt and pepper to taste; keep warm.

Cut each piece of venison into 3 slices. Spoon pumpkin polenta onto 4 plates, dividing evenly. Arrange venison pink side up on top of polenta. Strain pears; lean 1 piece of pear against each piece of venison. Drizzle plates with sauce; garnish with diced pumpkin and thyme sprigs.
Makes 4 servings

Forelle pears are small and sweet-tasting with a crisp texture. Quick-cooking polenta takes much less time to prepare than regular polenta and tastes just as good; look for it in specialty food stores.

GINGERBREAD MEN

4-1/2 cups (1.125 L) flour
2 tsp (10 mL) ground allspice
2 tsp (10 mL) ground cinnamon
2 tsp (10 mL) ground ginger
2 tsp (10 mL) baking soda
1/3 cup (75 mL) whipping cream
1/3 cup (75 mL) corn syrup
1 egg
2 tbsp (25 mL) molasses
1 cup (250 mL) butter, softened
1 cup (250 mL) packed brown sugar
Icing

In a medium bowl, whisk together flour, allspice, cinnamon, ginger and baking soda; set aside. In a 1 cup (250 mL) glass measure, beat together cream, corn syrup, egg and molasses. In a large bowl and using an electric mixer (preferably a stand mixer), beat butter and sugar together until light and fluffy. Beat in cream mixture until smooth; gradually beat in flour mixture until well combined and a smooth dough forms (dough will be quite soft). Divide dough into 4 even pieces; pat each into a disk. Wrap separately in plastic wrap; refrigerate for 1 to 2 hours until firmer but still soft enough to roll. If refrigerated longer, let dough stand at room temperature for 1 hour or until soft enough to roll.

Preheat the oven to 350°F (180°C). Line a large baking sheet with parchment paper. On a lightly floured surface, roll out 1 piece of dough to 1/4 inch (5 mm) thickness. Using a 5 inch (12 cm) gingerbread cutter, cut out gingerbread men, re-rolling trimmings once. Arrange 1 inch (2.5 cm) apart on baking sheet. Bake for 8 to 10 minutes until lightly browned around the edges. Let cool on baking sheet for 5 minutes; transfer to a wire rack to cool completely. Repeat with remaining dough. Decorate using your favourite icing.
Makes 40 gingerbread men

This recipe makes a whole army of gingerbread men but the dough keeps well in the refrigerate for up to 1 week so you'll be ready any time to bake up a batch of treats for all the kids in your life. Use your favourite icing to decorate the cookies.

TRADITIONAL MINCEMEAT TARTS

Mincemeat:

1 orange

1 lemon

8 oz (250 g) Northern Spy apples, cored and
chopped but not peeled (2 or 3)

3/4 cup (175 mL) packed dark brown sugar

1/2 cup (125 mL) Thompson raisins

1/2 cup (125 mL) sultana raisins

1/2 cup (125 mL) currants

1/2 cup (125 mL) chopped mixed candied peel

1/2 cup (125 mL) chopped suet

1/4 cup (50 mL) slivered almonds

2 tsp (10 mL) ground allspice

1/4 tsp (1 mL) ground cinnamon

1/4 tsp (1 mL) grated nutmeg

3 tbsp (45 mL) brandy

Shortcrust Pastry:

1/2 cup (125 mL) cold shortening

1/2 cup (125 mL) cold butter

3 cups (750 mL) flour

1/2 tsp (2 mL) table salt

1/3 cup (75 mL) ice water

Mincemeat: Grate rind and squeeze juice from orange and lemon. In a large bowl, combine citrus rind and juice, apples, sugar, raisins, sultanas, currants, candied peel, suet, almonds, allspice, cinnamon and nutmeg; stir well. Refrigerate, covered, for 12 hours.

Preheat the oven to 275ºF (135ºC). Spoon mincemeat into an 11 x 7 inch (2 L) baking dish; cover loosely with foil. Bake for 3 hours, stirring occasionally, until hot, moist and fragrant. Remove from the oven; let cool completely, stirring occasionally. Stir in brandy; set aside.

Shortcrust Pastry: Cut shortening and butter into 1/4 inch (5 mm) cubes. In a large bowl, whisk together flour and salt. Add shortening and butter. With a pastry blender or two knives, cut fat into flour until mixture resembles coarse crumbs. Gradually stir in just enough water to make dough clump together. Gather dough into a ball; turn out onto a lightly floured surface. Divide dough in half; pat out each half to a 5 inch (12 cm) disk. Wrap each disk in plastic wrap; refrigerate for 20 minutes.

Preheat oven to 400ºF (200ºC). On a lightly floured surface, roll out a piece of dough to 1/4 inch (5 mm) thickness. With a 3-1/2 inch (9 cm) cookie cutter, cut 12 rounds from dough, reserving trimmings; fit rounds into a 12 cup greased muffin pan. Fill tarts with half of mincemeat, dividing evenly.

Using a 2-1/4 inch (5.5 cm) cookie cutter, cut out 12 rounds from remaining rolled pastry, re-rolling trimmings once if necessary. Dampen edges of undersides of rounds; use to top tarts, sealing edges well. With a small, sharp knife, cut a slit in top of each tart for steam to escape. Bake for 12 to 15 minutes until golden brown. Let cool in pan on wire rack for 10 minutes. Carefully remove tarts from pan. Repeat with remaining pastry and mincemeat. Sprinkle tarts with icing sugar; serve warm.
Makes 24 tarts

The from-scratch mincemeat filling makes these festive tarts the best you'll ever taste. Just don't forget to make a wish with your first bite!

NEW YEARS EVE

As the corks fly, anticipation, merriment and music are the order of the

evening. A Champagne toast to the end of a year and a culinary

celebration that is a culmination of everything achieved. There are

great expectations as I have pulled out the stops and created dishes

that excite the palate with a diverse range of flavours. As the beat

goes on, the old year's destiny is fulfilled, the clock strikes midnight

and the New Year is welcomed in.

SQUAB CHARTREUSE

Squab:

2 squab (about 12 oz/375 g each)

2 tbsp (25 mL) vegetable oil

1/4 cup (50 mL) diced carrot (1 small)

1/4 cup (50 mL) diced celery (half a stalk)

1/4 cup (50 mL) diced leek

(white part only of 1 small)

1/4 cup (50 mL) diced onion (half a small onion)

1 tsp (5 mL) tomato paste

1/2 cup (125 mL) red wine

4 cups (1 L) Chicken Stock (page 217)

2 tsp (10 mL) black peppercorns

3 juniper berries

1 bay leaf

Salt and pepper

Savoy Cabbage Confit:

Half small Savoy cabbage (about 1 lb/500 g)

3 cups (750 mL) Chicken Stock (page 217)

2 cups (500 mL) rendered duck fat, melted

2 cloves garlic, thinly sliced

10 black peppercorns

1 sprig rosemary

1 sprig thyme

1 bay leaf

Salt

Vegetable Border:

2 medium carrots (about 2 oz/50 g each)

One-quarter small rutabaga (about 6 oz/175 g)

One-quarter small butternut squash

(about 8 oz/250 g)

16 fine green beans (each approximately

4 inches/10 cm long)

Salt

Squab: With a small, sharp knife, cut breasts from squab keeping the skin intact; refrigerate, covered, until ready to cook. Cut legs and wings from squab.

In a large, deep skillet, heat vegetable oil over medium-high heat. Add squab carcasses, legs and wings; sear for 3 minutes, turning often, until golden brown. Remove bones from skillet; set aside. Reduce heat to medium; add carrot, celery, leek and onion to skillet. Cook, stirring often, for 3 minutes or until golden. Stir in tomato paste until well combined. Stir in wine; bring to a boil over medium-high heat, stirring to scrape any browned bits from bottom of skillet. Return squab bones to skillet, along with stock, peppercorns, juniper berries and bay leaf; bring to a boil. Reduce heat to medium-low; simmer, uncovered, for 1 hour, turning any unsubmerged squab bones after 30 minutes.

Strain contents of skillet through a fine sieve into a medium saucepan, discarding solids in sieve. Bring liquid to a boil over high heat. Reduce heat to medium-high; boil for 25 to 30 minutes until reduced to 1/3 cup (75 mL) and sauce is thick enough to coat the back of a spoon. Season with salt and pepper to taste. Pour into a small bowl; refrigerate, covered, until ready to serve.

Savoy Cabbage Confit: Discard loose outer leaves of cabbage; trim root end. Cut cabbage into 4 wedges but do not remove core. In a deep 10 inch (25 cm) skillet with a lid, arrange cabbage wedges like the spokes of a wheel with root ends toward the centre. Pour over chicken stock and duck fat; add garlic, peppercorns, rosemary, thyme, bay leaf and a pinch of salt. Bring to a boil over high heat. Reduce heat to low; cook, covered, for 45 to 60 minutes until cabbage is very tender, turning cabbage halfway through cooking time. Remove from heat; keep warm.

Vegetable Border: Meanwhile, peel carrots, rutabaga and squash. Cut each into 2 x 1/4 x 1/4 inch (5 cm x 5 x 5 mm) batons (you'll need about 32 of each vegetable). Trim beans; cut each crosswise in half. In a medium saucepan of boiling salted water, cook carrots and rutabaga for 2 to 3 minutes until tender-crisp; remove with a slotted spoon and immediately immerse in a bowl of ice water. Add butternut squash and beans to saucepan; cook for 1 minute until tender-crisp; remove with a slotted spoon and add to rutabaga and carrots. Drain vegetables well; spread out on a clean towel to dry.

To Assemble: In a small, good-quality, non-stick skillet, heat olive oil over medium-high heat. Sprinkle reserved squab breasts on both sides with salt and pepper to taste. Add squab breasts to skillet; sear for 4 minutes, turning once, until golden. Remove to a cutting board; let stand for 5 minutes. Remove skin from squab breasts; cut each breast lengthwise into thin slices. Remove cabbage from its cooking liquid, discarding liquid. Remove large outer leaves from each wedge; set aside.

To Assemble:
1 tbsp (15 mL) olive oil
Salt and pepper
Softened butter

Caramelized Onions:
12 pearl onions (about 4 oz/125 g)
2 tbsp (25 mL) butter
1 tsp (5 mL) packed brown sugar
4 Potato Galettes (page 66)
Rosemary sprigs

Set four 3 inch (8 cm) diameter, 1-1/2 inch (4 cm) deep metal rings on a small baking sheet; generously butter the inside of each. Arrange carrot, rutabaga, squash and beans vertically around inside edges of rings, alternating vegetables until inside edges are completely lined.

Arrange a layer of large, outside cabbage leaves in base of each ring, making a layer 2 or 3 leaves thick, trimming off thicker ribs with scissors and cutting leaves to fit if necessary. Top each with one-third of each squab breast. Top each portion of squab with about 2 tbsp (25 mL) of inside leaves of cabbage (it's easiest, although messy, to break the inside leaves of the cabbage into pieces with your fingers) and another one-third of each squab breast. Repeat these last 2 layers once. Finally, top each with another 2 or 3 large cabbage leaves, trimming as before. Press down firmly (molds will be very full). With a large, very sharp knife, trim vegetables flush with top of molds. Refrigerate for at least 2 hours.

Caramelized Onions: In a small saucepan of boiling water, cook pearl onions for 10 to 15 minutes until just tender when pierced with a slim knife. Drain well. When cool enough to handle, trim root and stem ends; peel onions. In a small skillet, melt butter over medium heat. Add onions and sugar; cook for 3 to 5 minutes, stirring often, until golden and caramelized. Season with salt and pepper to taste; keep warm.

To serve, using an egg lifter, put assembled chartreuses, still in their rings, in a steamer set over a large skillet of boiling water; steam for 15 to 18 minutes until a skewer inserted into centre of 1 of the chartreuses feels hot when touched to your tongue.

In a small saucepan, reheat sauce over medium heat. Set 1 chartreuse on each of 4 plates. Pressing gently on contents, carefully remove rings. Top each with a potato galette and 3 pearl onions. Drizzle plates with sauce; garnish with rosemary.
Makes 4 servings

It's easier to fill the molds for this unusual main course while the squab and cabbage are still warm. Look for rendered duck fat in quality butchers and specialty food stores.

LOBSTER-TOMATO DOMES

2 live lobsters (1-1/2 lb/750 g each)
1/4 cup (50 mL) chopped basil
1 tsp (5 mL) grated lemon rind
1 tsp (5 mL) olive oil
Salt and pepper
1 stalk celery, diced
1 small carrot, diced
1 small onion, diced
1 sprig thyme
4 medium yellow tomatoes
4 medium red tomatoes
1 envelope (7 g) unflavoured
powdered gelatine
Caviar
Chervil
Basil Oil (page 115)

Put lobsters in a large pot of boiling salted water; return to a boil. Reduce heat to medium; boil, covered, for 8 minutes. Remove lobsters; set aside until cool enough to handle. Set a medium bowl in a larger bowl of ice; use this to hold the lobster meat as you extract it. Break tails from lobsters. With sharp kitchen scissors, cut underside of tails lengthwise; use your thumbs to open up tail shell so you can extract the meat in 1 piece. Set tail shells aside. With a small, sharp knife, remove intestinal vein that runs lengthwise down tail meat. With a large knife, cut heads in half down centre; remove and discard head sac. Pick out and discard all of the soft, grey gills (dead men's fingers). Pick out any meat. Twist off claws and legs. Crack claws and knuckles with the back of a sturdy knife, taking care not to crush the meat; remove meat. Reserve shells. With kitchen scissors, snip open larger legs; pick out meat with a pick or skewer. Cut 6 crosswise slices from 1 lobster tail for garnish; dice all remaining meat. In a medium bowl, stir together diced meat, basil, lemon rind, oil, and salt and pepper to taste. Refrigerate, covered, for up to 24 hours.

Put reserved lobster shells in a large saucepan with enough water to cover them. Bring to a boil over high heat; boil for 2 minutes. Add celery, carrot, onion, thyme and 1/2 tsp (2 mL) each salt and pepper. Reduce heat to medium-low; simmer, partially covered, for 1 hour. Strain through a colander, discarding solids. Strain liquid through a fine sieve lined with a double layer of cheesecloth. Measure 2 cups (500 mL) stock (reserve remainder for use in another recipe, such as a fish soup); set aside.

Cut a small X in the bottom of each tomato. In a large saucepan of boiling water, blanch tomatoes for 30 seconds; remove with a slotted spoon and immediately immerse in a bowl of ice water. Remove from water; peel tomatoes, cutting out cores with a small, sharp knife. Cut each tomato into 8 wedges; remove seeds and cut away all the membranes that divide each seed chamber so that inside surface of each tomato wedge is smooth. Arrange cut sides down in a single layer on a clean towel to drain.

Pour 1/3 cup (75 mL) reserved stock into a 2 cup (500 mL) glass measure; sprinkle gelatine over surface. Let stand for 5 minutes until puffy. Meanwhile, in a small saucepan, bring remaining stock to a boil over high heat. Pour hot stock over gelatine mixture, whisking constantly until gelatine has completely dissolved. Let cool to room temperature.

Line base and sides of six 3/4 cup (175 mL) dome-shaped molds or custard cups with tomato pieces, arranging them perpendicular to base, alternating colours and fitting tomato pieces snugly in molds so there are no gaps. Season inside of each tomato-lined mold with salt and pepper to taste. Carefully spoon lobster mixture into molds, dividing evenly and pressing down firmly (tops of tomatoes will curl over filling so try not to disturb tomatoes when filling molds). Spoon half of gelatine stock over lobster mixture, dividing evenly. Refrigerate molds and remaining stock for 2 hours or until lobster mixture is firm.

Quickly dip base of each mold in hot water; unmold onto a wire rack set over a shallow dish, shaking molds gently to release each dome. Top each with a slice of lobster. Put glass measure containing reserved stock in a small saucepan of simmering water; stir until melted but still syrupy. Carefully spoon stock over each lobster dome to glaze it. Refrigerate for at least 1 hour to set. Transfer to plates. Garnish with caviar, chervil and basil oil. *Makes 6 servings*

These stunning appetizers enclosing fresh lobster salad in a tomato shell are surprisingly simple to make.

FRESH OYSTERS

with Champagne Sabayon & Caviar

24 fresh oysters

Wilted Spinach:
1 tbsp (15 mL) olive oil
1 tbsp (15 mL) finely chopped shallot
1/4 tsp (1 mL) minced garlic
8 cups (2 L) lightly packed baby spinach leaves
Pinch grated nutmeg
Salt and pepper

Champagne Sabayon:
1/2 cup (125 mL) whipping cream
3 egg yolks
1/4 cup (50 mL) Champagne
1 tbsp (15 mL) lemon juice
Pinch cayenne
Pinch salt
Coarse salt and black peppercorns
1/4 cup (50 mL) caviar
24 parsley leaves

Scrub oysters well, paying attention to the hinge end where sediment can collect. Wearing a thick oven mitt, hold 1 oyster on work surface flat shell up; push the tip of an oyster knife into the hinge. With gentle force, press down diagonally, twisting the knife slightly to pry shells apart. Slide knife between shells, cutting oyster from top shell. Remove and discard top shell. Slide knife under oyster to release it from bottom shell; tip oyster and its juices into a small bowl. Rinse bottom shell; set aside. Repeat with remaining oysters. Cover and refrigerate oyster meat and reserved shells separately until ready to serve.

Wilted Spinach: In a large, non-stick skillet, heat oil over medium heat. Add shallot and garlic; stirring, for 3 to 5 minutes until softened but not brown. Increase heat to medium-high. Gradually add spinach; cook for 5 minutes, stirring gently and adding more spinach until all is wilted. Season with nutmeg, and salt and pepper to taste. Spoon spinach into a colander set over a bowl; let cool completely.

Champagne Sabayon: In a medium bowl, whip cream until stiff peaks form; set aside. In a deep, heatproof bowl and using a hand-held electric mixer, beat eggs yolks and Champagne until frothy.

Set bowl over a saucepan of simmering water; cook, beating constantly with electric mixer, for 8 to 10 minutes until sabayon is the consistency of softly whipped cream. Remove bowl from the heat; whisk in lemon juice, cayenne and salt. Fold in whipped cream until well combined and no white streaks remain.

Just before serving, preheat the broiler to high. Line a large serving platter with a 1/2 inch (1 cm) layer of coarse salt and sprinkle with peppercorns; set aside. Put reserved oyster shells on a large baking sheet. Spoon spinach into shells, dividing evenly. Top each with an oyster and some juices. Spoon Champagne sabayon over oysters, dividing evenly. Broil for 1 to 2 minutes until sabayon is golden. Arrange oyster shells on prepared platter. Garnish each with a little caviar and a parsley leaf.
Makes 24 hors d'oeuvres

I use French Fine de Claire oysters for this, but Malpeques or St. Simons from New Brunswick are also good choices. And to drink? The rest of the bottle of Champagne, of course. If you prefer, serve these as an appetizer, allowing 6 oysters per person.

TERRINE CONNAUGHT

with Cumberland Sauce

Terrine:

2 boneless duck magrets with skin
(1 lb 4 oz/625 g each)
1 duck leg (10 oz/300 g)
1 lb (500 g) boneless pork shoulder
8 oz (250 g) sliced boneless pork belly (rind removed before weighing)
3 tbsp (45 mL) port
1 tbsp (15 mL) Cognac
1/2 tsp (2 mL) pepper
1/8 tsp (0.5 mL) ground allspice
1/8 tsp (0.5 mL) ground cloves
1/8 tsp (0.5 mL) grated nutmeg
2 tsp (10 mL) butter
1/4 cup (50 mL) shelled natural pistachios
1 cup (250 mL) Duck Stock (page 217)
2 tsp (10 mL) unflavoured powdered gelatine
1 tsp (5 mL) salt
1/2 tsp (2 mL) baking soda
2 oz (50 g) foie gras, cut into thin strips
1 oz (25 g) drained black truffles, thinly sliced
1/4 cup (50 mL) dark rum

Cumberland Sauce:

1 orange
One-quarter lemon
1-1/2 cups (375 mL) red currant jelly
1/3 cup (75 mL) port
1 tsp (5 mL) mustard powder (such as Keen's)
1 tsp (5 mL) grated fresh ginger
1 tsp (5 mL) finely chopped shallot
Salad greens

Terrine: Carefully peel fat and skin from duck magret, using a sharp knife to release it if necessary. With a small, sharp knife held at a 45-degree angle, carefully cut fat from skin, discarding skin. Refrigerate fat; set magret aside.

Peel skin from duck leg, adding any loose pieces of fat to that reserved from magret. Using the method above, carefully cut fat from leg skin, discarding skin; add to magret fat. Cut duck leg meat away from bones, discarding bones; set meat aside.

Cut enough 1/2 inch (1 cm) crosswise strips from 1 magret to cover half of the base of a 6 cup (1.5 L) terrine or loaf pan. Cut remaining duck magret and leg into 1/2 inch (1 cm) chunks; put all duck meat in a medium, non-reactive bowl. Cut pork shoulder and belly into 1/2 inch (1 cm) chunks; put in a second medium, non-reactive bowl. In a small bowl, stir together port, Cognac, 1/8 tsp (0.5 mL) pepper, the allspice, cloves and nutmeg. Add half of port mixture to duck and half to pork; stir each mixture to coat well. Refrigerate, covered, for 24 hours for flavours to blend.

Remove strips of duck from bowl; pat dry with paper towels. Sprinkle with salt and pepper to taste. In a medium, good-quality, non-stick skillet, melt butter over medium-high heat. Add strips of duck; sear for 2 minutes, turning once, until browned on both sides. Remove to a plate; set aside to cool completely.

In a small saucepan of boiling water, blanch pistachios for 30 seconds; remove with a slotted spoon. Enclose pistachios in a clean towel; rub vigorously to remove skins. Pick off any remaining skin with your fingers, returning nuts to boiling water for a few seconds if skin is hard to remove. Set aside.

Pour 1/3 cup (75 mL) stock into a small bowl; sprinkle gelatine over surface. Let stand for 5 minutes until puffy. Meanwhile, in a small saucepan, bring remaining stock to a boil over high heat. Pour hot stock over gelatine mixture, whisking constantly until gelatine has completely dissolved. Let cool to room temperature.

Meanwhile, in a food processor, pulse uncooked duck meat using 6 to 8 one-second pulses until minced but not too fine. Remove to a large bowl. Pulse pork shoulder and belly using 4 to 6 one-second pulses until coarsely minced; add to minced duck in bowl. Add duck stock, salt, baking soda and remaining pepper; stir well. Check seasoning by frying a small spoonful of meat mixture in a small, good-quality non-stick skillet over medium heat until no longer pink inside. Taste this cooked piece and add more salt and pepper to raw mixture if necessary. Terrine should be well seasoned.

Spoon one-quarter of minced meat mixture over bottom of terrine or loaf pan, pressing down evenly. Top minced meat with alternate lengthwise rows of pistachio and foie gras, making 2 rows of pistachios and 2 rows of foie gras and using one-quarter of pistachios and one-quarter of foie gras for each row. Top with another quarter of minced meat, pressing down firmly to ensure meat is evenly distributed and taking care not to disturb rows of pistachios and foie gras. Top minced meat with alternate lengthwise rows of truffles and reserved seared duck meat, making 2 rows of truffles and 2 rows of duck meat and using one-half of truffles and one-half of duck meat for each row. Top with another quarter of minced meat, pressing down again and taking care not to disturb the other ingredients. Repeat pistachio/foie gras layer; top with remaining minced meat, pressing down again and taking care not to disturb the other ingredients. Terrine pan will be very full. Refrigerate, covered, for 24 hours for flavours to blend.

Meanwhile, cut reserved duck fat into 1/2 inch (1 cm) pieces. In a medium saucepan, stir together fat and 1/3 cup (75 mL) water. Cook, uncovered, over very low heat for 2 hours until fat is melted and cracklings have risen to the top. Strain through a fine sieve, discarding solids in sieve; refrigerate, covered, until ready to use.

Preheat the oven to 375°F (190°C). Cover terrine pan with a lid or tightly cover with foil. Set in a shallow roasting pan; pour boiling water into pan to come halfway up sides of terrine pan. Bake for 1-1/4 to 1-1/2 hours, until a meat thermometer inserted into centre of terrine registers 170°F (75°C). Increase oven temperature to 400°F (200°C); remove lid or foil from terrine. Cook for 10 to 15 minutes until just starting to brown.

Remove terrine from roasting pan; set on a wire rack. Immediately, pour rum over terrine. Let cool for 30 minutes. Put terrine pan in a shallow baking dish to catch any drips. Set a rectangular or oval dish slightly smaller than the pan on top of terrine; put 2 heavy, unopened cans or jars on top of dish to weight it down. Refrigerate for 24 hours.

In a small saucepan, heat reserved rendered duck fat over medium-low heat until completely melted. Pour evenly over terrine to cover it completely and fill pan to the brim (you may not need all the fat); refrigerate until set. For best flavour, let terrine mature for at least 1 to 2 days or up to 4 days before serving.

Cumberland Sauce: With a citrus zester, remove rind from whole orange and lemon quarter in long, thin strips, avoiding white pith.

In a small saucepan, heat jelly and port over medium heat until melted; stir in orange and lemon rind, mustard powder, ginger and shallot. Reduce heat to medium; simmer, stirring often, for 2 minutes for flavours to blend. Remove from heat; pour into a medium bowl. Let cool completely before serving.

Cut terrine into slices in pan or carefully turn out onto a cutting board before slicing. Serve with Cumberland sauce and salad greens.
Makes 10 to 12 servings

This rich terrine was a signature dish of chef Michel Bourdin when he presided over the kitchens of London, England's Connaught Hotel. Allow plenty of prep time as it takes at least 4 days but is well worth the effort. Duck magrets are the larger breasts from ducks raised to produce foie gras. Salted or unsalted pistachios are both fine for the terrine, but don't use the ones dyed red.

Maple-Glazed Duck Breast (recipe on page 213)

TIAN OF SALMON TARTARE

with Eggplant Confit

Eggplant Confit:

2 small tomatoes, cored, seeded
and quartered

4 cups (1 L) olive oil

1 cup (250 mL) balsamic vinegar

1 cup (250 mL) red wine vinegar

1/4 cup (50 mL) sherry vinegar

1 small onion, sliced

5 cloves garlic, halved

1 tbsp (15 mL) liquid honey

1 tsp (5 mL) salt

1 tsp (5 mL) mustard seeds

1/2 tsp (2 mL) pepper

1 sprig rosemary

1 sprig thyme

1 bay leaf

2 Italian eggplant (13 oz/400 g each; see note
below), trimmed and cut crosswise into
1/2 inch (1 cm) slices

Salmon Tartare:

8 oz (250 g) boneless, skinless salmon fillet

1 tbsp (15 mL) finely chopped chives

2 tsp (10 mL) lemon juice

1 tsp (5 mL) grated lemon rind

1 tsp (5 mL) finely grated fresh ginger

1 tsp (5 mL) finely grated fresh horseradish root

1/2 tsp (2 mL) seeded and minced hot
red chili pepper

Dash Worcestershire sauce

Dash Tabasco sauce

Salt

Cucumber ribbons and balls

Sour cream

Salmon caviar

Eggplant Confit: Cut tomato quarters crosswise into slices. In a large saucepan, stir together tomatoes, oil, balsamic, red wine and sherry vinegars, onion, garlic, honey, salt, mustard seeds, pepper, rosemary, thyme and bay leaf; bring to a boil over high heat. Reduce heat to medium-low; simmer for 10 minutes to blend flavours. Add eggplant, stirring to coat completely in oil mixture. Increase heat to medium; simmer, covered, for 8 to 10 minutes, stirring once or twice, until eggplant is tender when pierced with a slim knife but not overcooked. Remove from heat; let cool completely. Refrigerate, covered, for 24 hours. Let stand at room temperature for 2 hours before serving.

Salmon Tartare: Trim off all grey fat from salmon; dice salmon finely. In a medium bowl, stir together salmon, chives, lemon juice and rind, ginger, horseradish, chili pepper, Worcestershire and Tabasco sauces, and salt to taste. Season with more Worcestershire and Tabasco sauces, and salt if necessary.

With a slotted spoon, remove 12 slices of eggplant from confit. Put in a colander set over a bowl; let drain for 15 minutes. With a slotted spoon, transfer remaining eggplant to a food processor or blender. Stir oil mixture; add 1/2 cup (125 mL) to food processor, discarding herbs sprigs and remaining oil mixture. Pulse until smooth.

Set a 3 inch (8 cm) diameter metal ring or cookie cutter on 1 of 4 plates. Place a piece of eggplant in ring; top with one-eighth of salmon tartare. Repeat layers once; top with a piece of eggplant. Gently push ingredients onto plate, removing ring. Repeat with remaining ingredients and plates. Drizzle plates with some of the puréed eggplant confit; garnish with cucumber ribbons and balls, sour cream and salmon caviar.
Makes 4 servings

It's important that the eggplants for this fabulous layered appetizer measure no more than 3 inches (8 cm) in diameter. The recipe makes a big batch of puréed eggplant dressing but it can be stored in the refrigerator for several days. Use it to dress all your favourite salads or serve as a dip with crudités.

MAPLE-GLAZED DUCK BREAST

with Sweet Potato Purée & Glazed Apple

Duck Sauce:

2 lb (1 kg) duck bones, skin and fat removed

1 carrot, coarsely chopped

1 Granny Smith apple, coarsely chopped

1/3 cup (75 mL) coarsely chopped shallots

1 clove garlic, peeled

1/2 cup (125 mL) white wine

1 tsp (5 mL) tomato paste

2 sprigs thyme

1/2 cup (125 mL) Calvados

2 cups (500 mL) Veal Stock (page 216)

1 cup (250 mL) apple juice

1 tbsp (15 mL) butter, softened

Salt and pepper

Sweet Potato Purée:

2 medium sweet potatoes (12 oz/375 g each)

Salt

2 tbsp (25 mL) maple syrup

1 tbsp (15 mL) butter

Pepper

Glazed Apple:

1 Granny Smith apple

1 tsp (5 mL) icing sugar

Maple-Glazed Duck:

2 boneless duck magrets with skin
(about 1 lb 4 oz/625 g each)

Salt and pepper

3 tbsp (45 mL) maple syrup

Steamed Swiss chard

Duck Sauce: Preheat the oven to 400°F (200°C). In a shallow roasting pan, combine duck bones, carrot, apple, shallots and whole clove of garlic; roast for 30 minutes, stirring occasionally, until golden. With a slotted spoon, remove bones, vegetables and apple to a large saucepan. Pour off and discard excess fat from roasting pan; add wine to roasting pan. Bring to a boil over high heat, stirring to scrape up any browned bits from bottom of pan. Pour into saucepan; add tomato paste and thyme. Bring to a boil over high heat; boil for 3 minutes, stirring occasionally, until wine has almost all evaporated. Stir in Calvados; boil for 3 minutes until Calvados has almost evaporated. Stir in veal stock and apple juice; bring to a boil. Reduce heat to medium-low; simmer, partially covered, for 2 hours. Strain through a large colander into a large bowl; discard solids. Strain stock through a fine sieve into a medium saucepan. Bring to a boil over high heat. Reduce heat to medium-high; boil for 5 to 7 minutes until reduced to 3/4 cup (175 mL) and sauce is thick enough to coat the back of a spoon. Remove from heat; whisk in butter until melted. Season with salt and pepper to taste; keep warm but do not boil.

Sweet Potato Purée: Peel potatoes; cut 1 in half crosswise. With a mandolin slicer, cut 4 very thin slices from cut potato; pat slices very dry on paper towels. In a deep-fat fryer and following manufacturer's instructions, heat vegetable oil to 350°F (180°C). Alternatively, pour oil into a large, wide pot to a depth of 2 inches (5 cm); heat over medium-high heat until a candy thermometer registers 350°F (180°C). If using a pot, reduce heat as necessary to maintain correct temperature. Cook sweet potato slices in oil for 1-1/2 to 2 minutes until crisp. Remove with a slotted spoon; drain on a paper-towel-lined plate. Season with salt to taste.

Cut all remaining sweet potatoes into large chunks. In a large saucepan of boiling salted water, cook potatoes for 10 to 15 minutes until tender; drain well. In a food processor, pulse potato, maple syrup, butter, and salt and pepper to taste until smooth. Return to saucepan; keep warm.

Glazed Apple: Preheat the broiler to high. Peel, core and quarter apple. Trim each quarter so that the core area becomes a flat surface. With a small, sharp knife, cut a crosshatch pattern in flat surface of each apple quarter. Put apple quarters on a foil-lined baking sheet; sift icing sugar over each apple quarter. Broil 4 inches (10 cm) from heat for 3 minutes until apples are golden, watching carefully to prevent burning.

Maple-Glazed Duck Breasts: Preheat the oven to 400°F (200°C). Trim excess fat from magrets, lifting skin from edges of breasts to cut away any large pieces of fat. With a small, sharp knife, cut through skin and fat of breasts to make a crosshatch pattern, avoiding cutting into flesh; sprinkle both sides of breasts with salt and pepper. Heat a large ovenproof skillet over high heat. Add duck breasts skin side down. Lower heat to medium-high; sear for 5 minutes until golden. Turn breasts over; sear for 2 minutes. Drain off all fat from skillet. Brush skin of each breast generously with maple syrup. Transfer skillet to oven; cook for 10 to 15 minutes until a meat thermometer inserted into thickest duck breast registers 140°F (60°C). Remove duck breasts to a cutting board; tent with foil and let stand for 5 minutes. Slice thinly on the diagonal. Divide sweet potato purée among 4 plates; top with Swiss chard. Fan out slices of duck breast on each plate, dividing evenly. Spoon sauce around edges of plates; garnish with sweet potato chips and glazed apple.

Makes 4 servings

I like to use meaty duck magrets for this hearty winter dish. Ask your butcher to save some duck bones for you, or use the carcass and leg bones from a 4 lb (2 kg) duck.

COULIBIAC OF SALMON

Crêpes:

1 cup (250 mL) flour

1 cup (250 mL) milk

2 eggs, beaten

1 tbsp (15 mL) butter, melted

1 tsp (5 mL) finely chopped chervil

1 tsp (5 mL) finely chopped chives

1/4 tsp (1 mL) salt

1/4 tsp (1 mL) pepper

Vegetable oil

Filling:

2 lb (1 kg) piece boneless, skinless
Atlantic salmon fillet

2 egg whites

1/4 cup (50 mL) whipping cream

Salt and pepper

3 tbsp (45 mL) raw wild rice, cooked
(about 1/2 cup/125 mL cooked)

2 tbsp (25 mL) raw long-grain rice, cooked
(about 1/2 cup/125 mL cooked)

1 tbsp (15 mL) chopped chervil

1 tbsp (15 mL) chopped chives

1 tbsp (15 mL) chopped parsley

1 tbsp (15 mL) olive oil

2 cups (500 mL) quartered button mushrooms
(approximately 6 oz/175 g)

1 tbsp (15 mL) finely chopped shallot

8 quail eggs

6 cups (1.5 L) lightly packed baby spinach leaves

Crêpes: Put flour in a medium bowl; make a well in centre. In a small bowl, beat milk and eggs. Gradually beat milk mixture into flour until smooth. Strain through a fine sieve into a medium pitcher but don't force any residue through sieve. Stir in butter, chervil, chives, salt and pepper. Lightly oil a good-quality, 10 inch (25 cm), non-stick skillet (measured across the bottom); heat over medium-high heat until sizzling. Stir batter well. Pour about 1/3 cup (75 mL) batter into skillet, swirling to coat entire base evenly. Cook for 1 minute until golden on the underside. Flip crêpe; cook for 30 to 60 seconds until golden. Remove to a plate. Repeat with remaining batter, re-oiling skillet as necessary, to make 3 crêpes (you may not need all the batter); stack crêpes on plate as each cooks, interweaving layers with parchment paper. Let cool completely.

Filling: Trim 1-1/2 inches (4 cm) from each end of salmon (you'll need about 6 oz/175 g trimmings); set trimmings aside. Cut salmon fillet in half lengthwise; cover and refrigerate. Chop trimmings coarsely. In a food processor, pulse trimmings, egg whites, cream, and salt and pepper to taste until smooth and fluffy. Scrape this salmon mousse into a small bowl. In a medium bowl, stir together wild and long-grain rice, 1/3 cup (75 mL) salmon mousse, the chervil, chives, parsley, and salt and pepper to taste. Cover and refrigerate rice mixture and remaining salmon mousse.

In a large skillet, heat oil over medium heat. Add mushrooms; cook, stirring, for 5 to 7 minutes until golden and tender. Stir in shallot; cook, stirring often, for 3 to 5 minutes until shallot is softened but not brown. Spoon into a fine sieve set over a bowl; let cool completely. Discard any liquid in bowl. In a food processor, pulse mushroom mixture until finely chopped; scrape into a small bowl. Season with salt and pepper to taste; cover and refrigerate. Meanwhile, put quail eggs in a small saucepan of simmering water. Bring back to a simmer. Cook for 3 minutes; drain. Immediately cool under cold running water. Remove shells; refrigerate eggs.

Wash spinach; drain well. In a large, non-stick skillet over medium heat, cook spinach in water clinging to it for 5 to 7 minutes, turning occasionally, until all is just wilted. Remove from skillet with tongs; spread out on a clean towel to cool completely.

To Assemble: In a small bowl, beat egg with 1 tbsp (15 mL) cold water. Line a very large baking sheet with 2 sheets of parchment paper. On a lightly floured surface, roll out half of puff pastry to a 15 x 9 inch (38 x 23 cm) rectangle. Transfer to one-half of prepared baking sheet. Repeat with remaining pastry, arranging second piece alongside first and overlapping 2 long edges by 1/4 inch (5 mm) to make 1 rectangle approximately 18 x 15 inches (45 x 38 cm). Brush egg mixture over edges of pastry where they join; roll join with rolling pin to seal.

To Assemble:

1 egg

1 pkg (397 g) frozen puff pastry, thawed

Salt and pepper

Champagne Sauce (page 38)

2 tbsp (25 mL) finely chopped fennel fronds

Fennel fronds

Arrange crêpes across centre of pastry, parallel to long sides and overlapping them slightly. Spread one-third of spinach across centre of crêpes so area covered by spinach is roughly the same width and length as one piece of salmon. Top spinach with one-third of the salmon mousse, spreading thinly and evenly with a spatula. Lay one piece of salmon on top; sprinkle generously with salt and pepper.

Using your fingers, pile rice mixture on top of salmon, spreading evenly to cover salmon completely. Arrange quail eggs lengthwise along centre of rice, pressing in gently; sprinkle generously with salt and pepper. Again with your fingers, pile mushroom mixture over rice along each side of line of quail eggs (eggs should still be visible). Arrange another one-third spinach over mushrooms and eggs, pressing down gently so that spinach adheres. Spread one-third of mousse on the second piece of salmon to cover one side completely; place mousse side down on spinach, arranging it so that thicker side of 1 piece of salmon lies over thinner side of other. Press down gently. Spread remaining mousse evenly over top of salmon; sprinkle generously with salt and pepper. Cover evenly with remaining spinach.

Carefully fold crêpes over filling. Fold over 1 long side of pastry to enclose filling; brush top edge with egg mixture. Brush remaining pastry edges with egg mixture. Fold other long side of pastry over filling, pressing edges to seal well. Fold in ends of pastry, forming 1 end into a rounded "fish-head" shape and the other into a "tail" shape, if you wish, and sealing all edges with egg mixture. Reserve any pastry trimmings and remaining egg mixture. Refrigerate for at least 30 minutes.

Preheat the oven to 400°F (200°C). Carefully turn over the coulibiac on the baking sheet by lifting it by the top sheet of parchment then gently rolling it onto the lower piece so that the seam is underneath. Cut circles for eyes and pieces for mouth, gills and fins from pastry trimmings. With tips of a pair of sharp kitchen scissors, snip pastry along length of coulibiac to resemble "scales." Mark tail end with the tines of a fork. Brush coulibiac all over with remaining egg mixture. Bake for 35 to 40 minutes until pastry is puffed, golden brown and crisp. Let stand for 10 minutes before cutting crosswise into slices.

Meanwhile, in a small saucepan, reheat Champagne sauce but do not boil. Remove from the heat; stir in chopped fennel fronds. Arrange slices of coulibiac on plates. Drizzle sauce over plates; garnish with fennel fronds. *Makes 8 to 10 servings*

If you're entertaining a large number of people, this pastry-wrapped salmon with its rich filling of mushroom duxelle, salmon mousse and quail eggs makes a wonderful centrepiece. For the most tender wild rice, soak it for 24 hours in a bowl of cold water before draining and cooking according to the directions on the package.

CHEF'S PANTRY

Here are some basic recipes for stocks and other essentials that I like to keep handy in my kitchen.

Fish Stock

To achieve a good, clear fish stock, use only the bones, heads and trimmings from white fish for this recipe (red snapper and grouper are both good choices), avoiding any oily fish, such as salmon or mackerel.

In a large pot or Dutch oven, heat butter over medium heat. Add fish bones; cook, stirring, for 3 to 5 minutes until flesh adhering to bones is flaky but bones are not browned. Add wine; bring to a boil over high heat. Boil for 6 to 8 minutes until liquid has reduced by half. Add water; bring to a boil. As liquid comes to a boil, with a small strainer or large spoon, skim off the scum that rises to the top. Add celery, shallots, mushrooms, parsley, peppercorns, thyme and bay leaves. Reduce heat to low; simmer gently, partially covered, for 20 minutes, skimming occasionally. Strain stock through a large colander into a large bowl; discard solids. Season with salt and more pepper to taste. Let stock cool to room temperature; refrigerate, covered, overnight. Remove and discard fat from surface of stock. In a large saucepan, warm stock slightly to liquefy; strain stock through a fine sieve into airtight containers. Refrigerate for up to 3 days or freeze for up to 3 months.
Makes 7 cups (2.75 L)

Court Bouillon

This flavourful stock is indispensable in my kitchen for poaching seafood.

In a large stock pot, stir together water, wine, vinegar, onion, celery, carrot, lemon, bay leaves and star anise. Bring to a boil over high heat. Reduce heat to medium-low; simmer, uncovered, for 20 minutes for flavours to blend. Strain through a colander, discarding solids; pour into airtight containers. Refrigerate for up to 3 days or freeze for up to 3 months.
Makes 16 cups (4 L)

Beef or Veal Stock

If using the stock to make jus (recipe opposite), don't add any salt.

In a large stock pot, combine water and bones; bring to a boil over high heat. As liquid comes to a boil, with a small strainer or large spoon, skim off the scum that rises to the top. Add onion, carrot, celery, tomato paste, garlic, bay leaves, thyme and peppercorns. Reduce heat to low; simmer gently, partially covered, for 2 hours.

Strain stock through a large colander into a large bowl; discard solids. Season with salt and more pepper to taste. Let stock cool to room temperature; refrigerate, covered, overnight. Remove and discard fat from surface of stock. Strain stock through a fine sieve into airtight containers. Refrigerate for up to 3 days or freeze for up to 3 months.
Makes 12 cups (3 L)

Beef or Veal Jus

Beef or Veal Jus:
4 cups (1 L) beef or veal stock
Salt

In a medium saucepan, bring stock to a boil over high heat. Adjust heat so stock boils but doesn't splatter; boil for 20 to 45 minutes, until reduced to about 1 cup (250 mL). Season with salt to taste. Remove from heat; let cool completely. Pour into an airtight container; refrigerate for up to 3 days or freeze for up to 3 months.
Makes 1 cup (250 mL)

Chicken Stock

Chicken Stock:
4 lb (2 kg) chicken backs, necks or wings

Follow the recipe for beef stock using chicken pieces, and omitting the tomato paste.
Makes 12 cups (3 L)

Duck Stock

Duck Stock:
4 lb (2 kg) duck backs, necks or wings

Follow the recipe for beef stock using duck pieces, omitting the tomato paste and roasting the bones and vegetables first as follows: Preheat the oven to 400°F (200°C). Put bones, fat and trimmings in a shallow roasting pan, along with onion, carrot, celery and garlic. Roast, uncovered, for 30 minutes until starting to brown. With a slotted spoon, remove bones and vegetables to a large stock pot. Pour off and discard excess fat from roasting pan; add 1 cup (250 mL) water. Bring to a boil over high heat, stirring to scrape up any browned bits from bottom. Pour into stock pot with remaining water; continue as for beef stock.
Makes 12 cups (3 L)

Oven-Dried Plum Tomatoes

Oven-Dried Plum Tomatoes:
5 small plum tomatoes

Preheat the oven to 250°F (120°C). Cut tomatoes lengthwise into quarters; cut out tough stem ends. Arrange cut sides up on a wire rack set on a baking sheet. Bake for 2 hours, until shriveled but still moist. Let cool completely. (Oven-dried tomatoes can be refrigerated, tightly covered, for up to 2 days.)
Makes 20 pieces

Crème Fraîche

Crème Fraîche:
1 cup (250 mL) whipping cream
2 tbsp (25 mL) buttermilk (shake well before opening)

In a 2 cup (500 mL) glass measure, whisk together whipping cream and buttermilk. Cover tightly. Let stand at room temperature for about 24 hours, until thickened. Refrigerate, covered, for up to 1 week.
Makes 1 cup (250 mL)

Pastry Cream

Pastry Cream:
3 egg yolks
1 cup (250 mL) milk
1/4 cup (50 mL) sugar
3 tbsp (45 mL) cornstarch
Pinch table salt
1/2 tsp (2 mL) vanilla

Beat egg yolks in a medium bowl. In a small saucepan, whisk together milk, sugar, cornstarch and salt until smooth. Bring to a boil over medium-high heat, whisking constantly. Whisk about one-third of milk mixture into egg yolks; return yolk mixture to saucepan. Cook over medium-low heat, whisking constantly, for 3 to 5 minutes until pastry cream is thickened and smooth (do not boil). Remove from the heat; strain through a fine sieve into a medium bowl; stir in vanilla. Let cool to room temperature; whisk well until smooth. Lay a piece of plastic wrap directly on surface of pastry cream; refrigerate until chilled.
Makes 2 cups (500mL)

THE GRANITE PROJECT TEAM

It is the synergy of many that brings an idea to life. The synergy for the Granite Club Cookbook, *Capturing the Spirit*, included a dedicated group of Granite staff, professional graphic designers, photographers, a food writer and recipe tester, and the tremendous support of the Board of Directors.

Nigel Didcock: Executive Chef with more than 25 years of experience with Michelin and Relais & Châteaux establishments including the Connaught in London, Troisgros in France and Langdon Hall in Cambridge, Ontario. Granite Club 2003.

Stewart Reid: Executive Sous Chef with more than 20 years experience including Ménage á Trois in London, Langdon Hall, Oliver's Bistro and the Sutton Place Hotel. Granite Club 2003. (1)

Ian Rodger: Banquet Sous Chef with more than 20 years experience including the Four Seasons Inn-on-the-Park, Le Meridien King Edward Hotel, Expo '86 in Vancouver and the Sutton Place Hotel. Granite Club 2003. (2)

Greig King: Sous Chef with more than 16 years experience including the Sutton Place Hotel and Le Meridien King Edward Hotel. Granite Club 2003. (3)

Robert Locock: Sous Chef with more than 18 years experience including the Hilton Lodge Hotel, Castle Hotel Windsor, Ritz Carlton St. Thomas, the Millennium Mayfair and Millennium Knightsbridge in London. Granite Club 2004. (4)

Ashton Root: Sous Chef with more than 10 years experience including an apprenticeship at the Westin Prince Hotel and professional development with Laurent Cesne and Reynald Donet in France. Granite Club 2000. (5)

James Tesoro: Junior Sous Chef with over 10 years experience including Centro, Jump, Biff's, Café Brussels, the Sutton Place Hotel. Granite Club 2003. (6)

Renato del Sol: Pastry Chef with more than 22 years experience including the Manila Hotel and Makati Shangri-La in the Philippines. Granite Club 2006. (7)

Sarah Bassels: Food and Beverage Coordinator with more than 12 years experience including Muskoka Catering, Muskoka Lakes and Navigation in Gravenhurst. Sarah is a graduate of University of Guelph Hospitality Program. Granite Club 2002. (8)

Mary Elizabeth Sullivan: Assistant General Manager, project liaison and editor with more than 25 years communications and marketing experience in the private club industry. Granite Club 1996. (9)

Peter Fyvie: General Manager, with more than 40 years of experience in the hospitality industry including management positions in some of the finest hotels and restaurants in New York City, Bermuda and Toronto. Granite Club 1991.

Heather Cooper: Creative director, project manager and director of photography with over 40 years experience. Heather is a partner in the firm of Cooper Graham and author of Carnaval Perpetual. (9)

Julia Aitken: Food writer, recipe editor and wrangler with more than 25 years experience; author of three best-selling cookbooks and contributor to many major Canadian magazines. (10)

Eric Graham: Creative director, designer and director of photography with more than 12 years experience. Eric is a partner in the firm of Cooper Graham–creators of high-profile publications and originators of a major Canadian magazine. (11)

Vince Noguchi: Photographer with more than 25 years experience specializing in food & beverage and lifestyle photography. His images have appeared in cookbooks and many major Canadian magazines. (12)

Sandy Nicholson: Photographer with more than 10 years experience, specializing in people and lifestyle photography, and has contributed to many major Canadian magazines and corporate publications. (12)

7

8

INDEX

Unless otherwise stated in the recipes, the following assumptions are made about ingredients:

- Butter is unsalted and cold
- Citrus juice is freshly squeezed
- Eggs are large and at room temperature
- Flour is all-purpose and unbleached
- Herbs are fresh
- Milk is 2%
- Olive oil is extra virgin
- Parmesan is freshly grated from a block of cheese
- Parsley is Italian flat-leaf
- Pepper is white and freshly ground
- Salt is coarse kosher
- Sugar is granulated

GRANITE
C L U B

Copyright © 2007 by the Granite Club
Photographs © 2007 Vince Noguchi & Sandy Nicholson

Published by the Granite Club
Toronto, Canada

Book purchases and inquiries: kitchen@graniteclub.com

ISBN 978-0-9783936-0-1

Printing: Options Graphic Management Ltd.
Printed in China

Prepress: C.J. Graphics Inc.

Recipe Development and Food Styling: Nigel Didcock

Recipe Editing and Testing: Julia Aitken

Creative Direction, Book Design, Art Direction and
Project Management: Heather Cooper & Eric Graham

a
Cooper
Graham
book